SPORTS & LEISURE CLUB MANAGEMENT

A Handbook for Organisers

Andrew Sceats

MACDONALD AND EVANS

Macdonald & Evans Ltd
Estover, Plymouth PL6 7PZ

First published 1985

© Macdonald & Evans 1985

British Library Cataloguing in Publication Data

Sceats, Andrew
        Sports and leisure club management: a handbook
for organisers.
1. Recreation centers—Great Britain—Management
I. Title
790'.06'9   GV75

ISBN 0–7121–0665–0

Typeset by J & L Composition Ltd,
Filey, North Yorkshire
Printed in Great Britain by
Hollen Street Press Ltd,
Slough

SPORTS & LEISURE CLUB MANAGEMENT

For Vivian

Foreword

Sports clubs come in all shapes and sizes, but they share a number of common characteristics and face similar problems.

From the Sunday morning "pub" football club using facilities in a local park, to the large professionally run golf and country club—all must aim to be financially self-supporting.

They are dependent not only on the financial support of their members, but also on a vast pool of enthusiasm and voluntary effort that is the corner stone of a successful club. This effort needs harnessing and directing by club officials, some professional, some amateur, for a club to prosper and develop.

This book provides a useful point of reference for those officials already in the field and those trying to establish a new club. It draws together in an "easy to read" style, much useful advice for the club organiser on matters as diverse as design and finance, coaching and injuries.

The role of sports clubs in British sport cannot be under-estimated. In many sports, particularly team games, they provide the structure through which a novice can progress to a high level of performance. They form an essential base for the Sports Council in the promotion of "Sport for All". It is important to the Council that clubs are accessible to people from differing backgrounds and of varying abilities and that these clubs are well-organised so that people can experience the sense of achievement and enjoyment that so many already derive from participation in sport and physical recreation.

The sports club also plays its part as a community focal point and for many people becomes a major lifelong leisure interest and point of social contact.

Andrew Sceats has drawn on his experience in sports administration in this book to provide a much needed handbook for club organisers as they seek to manage and develop what is such an important part of the British sporting and leisure scene.

May 1985

JOHN WHEATLEY
DIRECTOR GENERAL, THE SPORTS COUNCIL

v

Acknowledgments

There is a vast army of unpaid volunteers who cheerfully and enthusiastically give their time, effort and money to helping their club organisation, and to the small part of this army that I have been in contact with I give my thanks for showing how problems can be faced and overcome.

Special thanks are due to Derek Dredge, Potters Bar Sports Club, Ian Buttress, Warrington Sports Club and James Dick, Wakefield Sports Club, who all gave me practical advice and valued hospitality. David Lloyd kindly let me view the computer facilities at his club.

Stephen Dover, Edward Grayson and John Jeffery were kind enough to advise me in the fields of accounting, sports law and management respectively. Research needs guidance and the staff of the Sports Council's publications department and Information Centre dealt with many of my requests with much attention and good humour.

Numerous commercial suppliers to clubs spent time answering my questions and they gave me an insight into club management from their side of the fence.

I would also like to express my gratitude to Mark Hannon whose excellent humour provided the cartoons for the book.

Finally, no manuscript can reach a publisher without being typed and I am indebted to Jenny Treacy for doing the job so well.

AS

Contents

CONTENTS

Introduction

Sports, sociability, substitutes, subscriptions, showers and sponsorship are some of the terms readily associated with sports clubs, including those organised on a voluntary basis. To those individuals responsible for running the affairs of sports clubs there are other terms which, while seeming more mundane, are often more familiar. These include—safety and security requirements, contract law, balance sheets, audited accounts and cash flow projections, rate relief, stretchers, planning permission and building regulations approval.

Although there is a growing body of literature dealing with sport and leisure topics, there has been a lack of easily understood material about sports clubs which is readily available to those most closely involved, the club officials themselves. To date, good work which has been carried out in other fields such as accountancy, the law and personnel management, has had to be applied to the organisation of sports clubs.

There are specialist sports organisations such as the Sports Council, the Central Council for Physical Recreation and the National Playing Fields Association which produce written material and offer advice but because of their differing natures, it is difficult for a club official to know which to approach about a specific problem. The purpose of this book is to provide, in a clear way, advice and recommendations to help overcome many of the difficulties which may arise.

Chapter One will examine the different ways in which a voluntary club may be constituted and how this can be achieved. The club as a charity, a limited company, or a non-profit making club with trustees are some of the options available. A specimen example of club rules and constitution is set out and the relationship between members and committees is examined. The organisation and procedures involved in holding meetings are described.

The key to the success of a club often lies in its financial well-being. Chapter Two will examine the items of expenditure which can be expected and the methods by which they can be minimised. Normal revenue-raising methods and their maximisation are also covered in full. A simplified balance sheet, statement of accounts and cash flow forecast is included, together with a glossary of common accounting terms.

Frequently, clubs are dependent on special fund raising events to enable them to maintain existing facilities or provide new facilities. Chapter Three describes the special nature of these events, such as tournaments, sponsored walks, horse race evenings, jumble sales etc., how they can be successfully staged and how common problems can be prevented or overcome. Other forms of fund raising such as sponsorship deals, the availability of assistance in the form of grants and loans from public sources and the help which can be obtained from commercial bodies are analysed.

The type and useage of facilities which are available to clubs are the subjects of Chapter Four. The needs of a club should be clear in the minds of club officials and every effort made to ensure that they are met in the most practicable and efficient way. General principles of design of clubhouses and pavilions are one of the main areas discussed. The implications to the club of facilities and their influence in encouraging or retaining members are covered.

The legal responsibilities which clubs have are set out in Chapter Five. Legislation could be applicable to almost every part of a club's activity. Basic requirements of planning, health and safety and employment laws and regulations among others are discussed. Pertinent civil cases are also mentioned. Although injuries and accidents at sports clubs are usually associated with the playing aspects it is often on the "non-sporting" side that these happen. Advice which is given in Chapter Six not only looks at preventative and curative means which are available but is concerned with how clubs can obtain advice from outside agencies.

Appendix A describes how two sports clubs with different aims, size and activities could be founded. The first is a multi-sport club in a city location; the other is a small village club. Many of the points made earlier will be brought together in this exercise.

Most of the topics covered in the six chapters are of sufficient complexity to merit a volume in their own right to do them full justice. In the circumstances, a list of reading references and useful addresses will be of interest to the reader.

It is not the intention of this book to launch into complex theories about sport and leisure and what motivates individuals and groups to participate. It should, however, be useful for clubs and their officials to recognise and understand that there are certain principles which should be taken into account when considering how a club functions. Perhaps the reason why some clubs are more successful than others is due to their recognition, whether consciously or unwittingly, of these principles.

Increased participation and interest in sport and leisure activities has been influenced by many factors, one of the most significant being the additional time available, whether due to earlier retirement, unemployment, "flexitime", or a deliberate four-day week. Sport is now being accepted as a fashionable way of spending spare time.

The benefits of improved health which exercise encourages has led to many people who would not have started activities such as jogging or aerobics in the past now becoming some of their most passionate devotees. Exercise has almost become a religion. Disciples now need a daily "fix", whether experiencing Jane Fonda's Workout, "pumping iron" in a bodybuilder's gymnasium or running long distances daily in preparation for a future marathon.

Media coverage of sports events and sports personalities, not only during their competition but in their private lives, has heightened public awareness of the sports world. Although a significant number of radio listeners and television viewers are apparently infuriated by the level of exposure which is afforded to special events such as the football World Cup or the Olympic Games, it is probable that they too participate in or are interested by another type of sport.

Many sports which have been televised extensively in recent years have seen their popularity rise at grass roots level. Examples of these include snooker, darts and gymnastics. Often this growth in interest is sustained, but it can be shortlived as seen with skateboarding. Demand for useage of public tennis courts mushrooms at the time of the Wimbledon Championships but thereafter declines dramatically.

Although it is difficult to accurately measure participation in most sports, mainly because a number of participants are not affiliated to the relevant governing body of sport, large increases have been recognised in:

— sports newly introduced, e.g. board sailing and microlight flying;
— sports which demonstrate real or apparent exclusivity, e.g. skiing;
— sports which can be completed in a short time, e.g. squash.

Changes in both fashion and the social climate have affected the popularity of sports. The growth of the martial arts such as judo, karate and kung fu has been influenced to some extent by the increase of violence, especially that shown towards women. Increasing numbers of women now attend self defence classes, many of which are organised by voluntary clubs.

Voluntary sports clubs have been described as being the backbone of British sport. They have become the envy of much of the world and have been the model which has been adopted especially in English speaking countries. While publicly owned facilities and those run by commercial operators allow sports to be tried out, it is more often that the voluntary clubs are able to offer high class competition.

Today's clubs are the result of a continuing development over the last 150 years. Their form of organisation and the benefits they bring have been recognised by government as fulfilling a social service. They have merited assistance which can be variable and take many forms—grants, loans, rate relief and gifts in kind being the most common.

As one would expect with at least 150,000 clubs catering for a wide range of sports activities, there is a corresponding variation in their size and appearance. Most clubs, however, have the following common features:

— a committee structure;
— acceptance of the rules of the sport;
— acceptance of the rules and conditions imposed on the members by the club.

The club should try to identify and satisfy the needs of the community of which it is a part. In a rural area a village club using the village green for cricket and football with a bar in a pavilion may be suitable. In an urban area with a larger population, the multi-sport club with more elaborate facilities may be able to meet more diverse demands.

Club committees should appreciate (and many do) that there are many reasons why members join. These include:

1. The provision of facilities to allow the participation in a sport by way of pitches, pavilions, courts etc.
2. The pleasure of competition which can be experienced.
3. The opportunity of improving a skill at a sport.
4. The opportunity of being able to mix socially.
5. The benefits of keeping fit.
6. The availability of positions of responsibility in the running of the club's affairs. Some people are able to experience this for the first time. To others it is an extension of the rest of their lives.

One of the strongest attracting features of voluntary clubs is their ability to allow sports and social activities to take place within a framework of complete democratic self-organisation and participation. It is the ability of club members to take their own decisions, normally through the committee system and the AGM, which encourages many to join. Although in many publicly and commercially organised facilities users are able to make an input, the important policy-making decisions, such as on pricing, are usually in the hands of an overall authority.

The corporate or "belonging" leisure activity is not a classless activity although this situation is being improved. It has been shown that members of the middle class are more likely than members of the working class to become members of sports clubs. The working class ethic is based on the shared community in the home or in the social club. This therefore deters from membership of sports clubs.

There are two types of barrier to people joining clubs. These are "economic" and "institutional". Economic barriers include the cost of travelling to the club, the level of subscription and the playing costs. Institutional barriers include the need for certain clothing, "whites only to be worn", and equipment to be used, adherence to club rules and conventions and the necessity to take part in customs and events, like the "Stag Dinner", organised at the club.

Although many keen sportsmen may say that sport to them is the most important recreational activity which can be undertaken, overall, sport is but one of many types of recreation. Other activities such as hobbies, TV, radio and audio, gardening and social outings have been measured as having more participants than sport. Clubs should realise that their image has to be made as attractive as possible so that competition in the form of alternative providers, i.e. the public and commercial sectors, and other types of leisure activity are met as successfully as possible. Money which could be spent at the club could be spent alternatively on a personal stereo system, also it is less hazardous to "kick" a football on a television screen during a video game than it is to chase the real thing on a muddy pitch in the middle of January. Also an individual could consider using a badminton court at a leisure centre rather than join a badminton club.

The standard of club officials varies as does the standard of the clubs they organise. Most officials are unpaid and give their time, and often money, freely to enable the club to function smoothly. Three factors which make officials' tasks more difficult are:

1. The demands of their everyday lives;
2. The often conflicting requirements of club members;
3. The need for the club to comply with outside requirements, e.g. the wide range of legislation which is now applicable to the club.

Lack of candidates for office in the club is a common situation and it leads to the workload falling on the shoulders of the willing few, normally the same willing few over a long period of years. This is a potentially dangerous situation which should be avoided if possible.

Sports club members are the same as other people in having expectations and aspirations to improve their, and the club's, situation. This is often achieved by the upgrading of existing facilities and the provision of new facilities. If this happens the club is placed on "The Treadmill of Improvement". As the new facilities are provided new members are needed to generate additional revenue and subsequently the new members will want new facilities and so on.

Voluntary clubs are similar to other types of organisation in that they are subject to the laws of the land. Modern legislation is very complex and unless one is a specialist, legislation requirements are difficult to understand let alone implement. But legislation affects clubs in the fields of finance, planning, health and safety, personal liability, employment, gambling, drinks licensing and many more. Many clubs own considerable assets and generate an annual turnover of thousands of pounds. Consequently the days when accounts could be produced on the back of a cigarette packet are long gone (or should be) and they are often comparable to those of a public company.

Not only should officials of the club be proficient in technical matters, as instanced above, or know of the availability of satisfactory advice which can be called upon, but they should also ensure that they are certain of the principles on which the club is organised and that these are being followed. Although this sounds daunting, it is probably the system which underlies committee meetings and the Annual General Meeting.

Voluntary clubs often act as a focal point in their community where people can meet and make their own decisions. They are also able to adapt quicker than other types of sports facility. The club should try to adopt a flexible approach when making decisions. It is not good enough for its committee to take a course of action simply because it has always done it that way. The methods adopted by competitors should be studied and if benefits can be deduced these should be applied.

This is a country where the voluntary ethos is greatly valued and it should be protected and encouraged in the sports world as elsewhere. If this book is able to help the vast army of volunteers who wear the badge "club official" in their necessary, but often unsung, work, its purpose will have been fulfilled.

It is perhaps appropriate that the best commendation for the work and role of voluntary sports clubs is contained in the 1982 Annual Report of The Sports Council of Wales—a land itself renowned for community spirit and self help—virtues which clubs also display:

> "The sports club is also a very important unit in increasing participation and without it sport would not exist in this country. It looks after and encourages excellence. It has to be dependent upon its own resources for the day to day running without any grant-in-aid and the £219,736 which the Council has given to help clubs to provide better facilities is a good investment for the future of sport in Wales."

1
Management of a Club

*"Please accept my resignation. I don't care to belong to any club that will
have me as a member."*
                                                                  Groucho Marx

Although the above quotation is often incorrectly used to describe an
application to join a club, it is interesting to note that it was used
when resigning as a member of a club.

STRUCTURE

Membership of clubs of all types with differing objectives is a common social phenomenon throughout the world. Clubs cater for all
ages, classes, tastes and creeds. If someone wants to carry out an
activity you can be sure there is a club he (or she) can join to further
his knowledge and enjoyment of this pursuit. Alternatively, if no club
exists and he is enthusiastic enough he can found his own club; with a
little publicity others of like mind will soon appear and join in.

Clubs are found everywhere—in schools, in the workplace, in local
community areas, as national institutes. Although the points made in
this, and the succeeding chapters are aimed specifically at sport and
recreation clubs, especially those run on a voluntary non-profit distributing basis, it is likely that the principles involved could be used in
other spheres.

There are many reasons why people join and become members of
clubs. These include:

— learning or improving a skill;
— benefitting from a social situation;
— meeting or beating a challenge;
— developing one's personality.

While clubs have developed primarily to provide facilities to conduct
an activity, they have also satisfied other desires either directly or
indirectly. For example, a club tournament which is staged will
allow some members to participate in the event directly as players or
officials, others will administer it both beforehand and while it takes

place, and another section will be attracted to the social side—watching the event or having a drink and perhaps something to eat in the clubhouse. A tournament is a good way to raise club funds and introduce it to outsiders, whether participants or casual (or invited) visitors.

Clubs vary in many respects. They can have a small membership or large; they can be predominantly male or female or of mixed composition; they can be competitive in outlook or very relaxed in approach; they can have a few facilities or many; they may be exclusive or open to all; they can specialise in one sport or contain many sections; they can appeal to the young or the old or to all age groups. The list is endless.

It is important, especially for club officials who are usually drawn from the club's members, that whatever the club's aims and however its affairs are managed, these are achieved in the best possible way both for existing and, if they are wanted, for potential new members. It is the ability to satisfy existing demand or stimulate expansion that is one of the hallmarks of a successful club.

Before looking at the different forms of club organisation which exist and examining their characteristics it would be useful to discuss in general four subjects which, while often being taken for granted, should be regarded as being crucial to the well-being and prosperity of a club. These are:

— club rules;
— management style of a club;
— organising and running meetings;
— committees and officers.

RULES

These should meet the current needs of the club's members and contain the facility to be altered to cover new circumstances as they arise, for example, if new members need to be admitted or if new sections are requested in a club.

The rules, often known as the constitution, of a club should be as concise as possible, easily understood by all and not open to misinterpretation. They should be attractively presented and in Chapter Two ideas will be given on additional information which could be included with the rules in a club handbook. They should not be oppressive and wherever possible not discriminate against any member or groups of members. Valid exceptions to this would be differential subscription rates—for instance a reduction for social, country, junior or senior members if the club members feel this appropriate. Rules should not condone illegal acts, and as will be seen in Chapter Five the sports club is now subject to an enormous range of legislation mainly of a civil nature. Above all rules should meet the standard of commonsense. Perhaps one of the most important jobs of a club's management committee would be to appoint someone always to keep the rules under scrutiny and if necessary recommend updating them when required. Also, club members while discussing them heatedly in the bar after an AGM may come up with a good idea which should be discussed and adopted.

In the body of the rules details of the following should be given:

— the name of the club;
— the club's location and when it was founded;
— the aims or objectives of the club;
— the method of election of members;
— the method of election of club committees and officers;
— the financial arrangements of the club such as method of charging, subscriptions levels, various powers of cheque signatories, borrowing responsibilities;
— the role of trustees (if any);
— the liability of the club towards its members in the event of theft, accident;
— the procedure to be followed if rules have to be altered, or revised;
— the situation if the club needs to be disbanded for any reason;
— the arrangements for annual general meetings and extraordinary general meetings;
— the procedures for committee meetings and the powers conferred on committees.

In addition to the items covered above it may be useful to include the following items:

— the colours or insignia of the club;
— the clothing to be worn or equipment to be permitted;
— the bye-laws of the club to deal with the behaviour of pets or children on the club's premises;
— the control of the bar, the permitted licensing laws and purchase of items by members and others;
— the governing bodies of sports and other organisations to which the club is affiliated.

MANAGEMENT STYLE

In Chapter Four a detailed study will be made of how clubs can best make use of their facilities and suggestions will be offered about the methods associated with attracting and retaining club members.

1. MANAGEMENT OF A CLUB

There is no doubt that the way a club presents itself can be a major determining factor in people's minds when they consider joining a club and using its facilities. The image which is conjured up can either agree with the perception of how they want the club to be or alter their own view of what a club should be. Because expectations vary, it is important for clubs to realise that the atmosphere which is developed may not be suitable to satisfy the needs of everyone. Some individuals are happy in spartan surroundings while others may wish for a more luxurious environment.

Sport and recreation are more about people than about facilities and it could be said that while the members are the club, the organisation of the club influences the attitude of its members, or a large proportion of them. Many clubs have demonstrated a knack of accommodating the unusual or eccentric as well as the average member; without this former type of member, clubs may lose their charm and their ability to appeal to all members of the public. In terms of ability, it is often the member who is seen to be apart from the mainstream who is the most talented performer.

A club with a sympathetic management style would demonstrate some of the following characteristics:

1. A friendly approach which does not become overbearing, e.g. club officials who are informally dressed.
2. A consistent approach towards members and their activities, e.g. rules being uniformly applied to all members with no "favouritism".
3. Encouragement of a good level of communication between members, e.g. the regular circulation of a newsletter with all members being invited to contribute.
4. A sense of responsibility towards the members which, if possible, should extend to their families and other non-members especially those affected by the club's activities, e.g. if a player is injured his progress should be monitored and help offered if hardship is suffered.
5. A businesslike way of conducting its affairs, primarily in the way it provides playing, and directly supporting, facilities for members, e.g. development plans should be made known to all members with the consequences pointed out.
6. A social atmosphere in which all members are given an opportunity to participate as fully as possible, i.e. no sections should be deliberately ignored.
7. An ability to understand the needs of members and to meet these where possible, e.g. in an area with high unemployment any members affected could have their subscriptions reduced, offered payment by instalment or substituted with work at the club.

1. MANAGEMENT OF A CLUB

ORGANISING AND RUNNING MEETINGS

Although very often the most heated debate about the affairs of a club is conducted in the bar after a match, the more appropriate forum should be properly convened meetings. These will be both small groups of members, who have delegated powers such as the management and bar committees, and at meetings which are open to all members, namely the annual general meeting to discuss routine matters, or the extraordinary general meeting where a specific subject is to be discussed.

The methods employed in arranging and conducting meetings are good indicators of how the club is generally run. If important papers are not circulated in time or insufficient notice of a meeting is given, this could show that not enough thought has been given to ensuring the smooth running of the meeting. On the other hand it may be that the club's officials may be new to the job, or the photocopier has broken down or a key person, say the club's secretary, has been unwell and has been unable to give his attention to the task in hand.

The club's members and officers should ask two key questions, firstly what is the purpose of the meeting and secondly is the machinery for fulfilling the purpose of the meeting satisfactory.

Meetings have several purposes:

1. To allow subjects to be debated; these range from the provision of a new expensive facility through to the need to change the after match refreshment from sandwiches to a cooked meal. If a subject is of interest to enough members it should be debated:
2. Participation in the decision making process allows members the right to show their interest in a club's activities in a responsible and constructive way.
3. To indicate to non-committee members that issues in the club are being dealt with in an organised way.
4. The fulfilment of requirements which may be inherent in a club's constitution.

It is important for the chairman of meetings to ensure that wherever possible all members have an opportunity to state their views, that certain members do not monopolise the discussion and that hesitant or new members are encouraged to make their contribution.

Although there is no legislation concerning the meetings of unincorporated sports clubs, it is important that club rules which are the contract between members are clear on several points concerning meetings. These are:

— categories of those members entitled to attend and vote are clearly defined;

— the rules concerning meetings are observed;
— the necessary quorum is present;
— the presence at meetings and duties of the chairman (and his substitute if necessary) are set out;
— the method of notifying members of meetings is clear and followed;
— voting procedures are set out;
— an appropriate venue for a meeting should be used.

Checklist 1: For a good meeting

1. It has been well advertised with members having sufficient time to prepare their contribution, if they want to make one.
2. The agenda will not be too long; a second meeting could deal with items not covered at the first meeting if necessary.
3. Documents should be circulated well before the meeting.
4. The venue is of sufficient capacity for those expected to participate with an error on the large side being preferable than being too small. It should allow everyone good visual contact with the chair.
5. Communication should be easy with aids being available e.g. microphones for all participants, slide projectors for demonstration purposes.
6. The timing of the meetings is important, for instance a football club annual general meeting will be more relevant during the season rather than in mid-July. Holiday periods should be avoided.
7. A sympathetic but firm chairman should be appointed who can guide discussions and ensure the meeting is finished in good time. It is recommended that the chairman is only able to exercise a vote in the event of a tied vote.
8. As many members as possible should be able to vote, those exempt could be juniors under sixteen or non-playing members.
9. Encouragement should be made for people to attend. A meeting could be preceded by a social event; free drinks could be offered.
10. The voting and telling procedure should be clear, it is normally best for a secret ballot to be held. A show of hands may be embarrassing for some members over a sensitive issue.
11. Debate should be carried out in an orderly fashion with language used being non-offensive. One person should speak at a time and the chairman should try to halt distracting talk from other quarters of the meeting. Motions should be proposed before discussion can begin and voted upon before the next item on the agenda is started.
12. It is advisable that a written record is kept of the discussion and

the ensuing recommendations and decisions taken. These are normally known as the minutes of a meeting. The signs of good minutes are that they are concise, accurate and capable of being understood by people not present at the meeting.

13. The chairman should ensure that time is not being wasted during discussion and if necessary propose a "guillotine" after a reasonable length of discussion time. Once repetition begins it is time for a vote to be taken.

14. During meetings outside distractions such as noise should be minimised as much as possible e.g. the bar could be temporarily closed.

15. If the above points are followed the meeting should be both better managed and enjoyed by those present. Also it is unlikely that there will be scope for members to be aggrieved and thus go to court about any decisions which have been taken.

COMMITTEES

Having recognised the **reasons** for holding meetings, the club should examine their existing committee structure to see if it is adequate to meet its task, for example it could be that when the club was established there was no licensed bar to be managed or perhaps the club did not own its playing facilities. If this situation is changed the club will need a bar committee, sometimes called a wine committee, and a ground committee.

The following committees may be constituted but the size, style and aims of a club will influence the need for committees:

— overall management;
— house;
— ground;
— bar;
— social;
— selection and coaching;
— finance;
— planning;
— sectional committees, e.g. football, squash etc.

In addition there can be subsidiary committees dealing with specific issues or sectional interests. These could include:

— tournament;
— publicity;
— juniors;
— ladies;
— catering.

1. MANAGEMENT OF A CLUB

The committees have different roles in the club's affairs and their main functions are outlined below.

The management or general committee
This is in overall charge of the club's activities especially the examination of the workings of the club in its totality. It monitors and plans the activities of the club.

Because of the complexities of running a club with sizeable assets and a large turnover, it should delegate specific activities to various sub-committees, so that day-to-day decisions can be made in an efficient manner. The management committee should liaise closely with the relevant sub-committee when taking any important decision. Financial decisions should only be taken when recommendations from the finance committee have been taken into consideration.

To ease communications, it would be prudent for each main sub-committee of the club to contain at least one member of the management committee. If a club has more than one sports section, each section should have a representative on the management committee. This will ensure that participants of all the different activities are able to have their views known. Although it could be argued that all sections should be equally represented, there may be a case for one sport having a disproportionate influence. Take the example of a soccer club starting a squash section, which is then successful and has a large growth of members with the consequence that the original members' views may be swamped. If a club wishes to found a new section, it should be aware that this is one of the possible consequences and the club rules should be framed to take care of this possibility.

Because the day-to-day running of the club's affairs has been delegated to other sub-committees, it should only be necessary for the management committee to meet, say, four times a year. If a major problem arises which needs urgent attention, the committee should be able to convene after reasonable notice.

The house committee
This should consist of one member from the management committee plus other members who can be persuaded to join. All buildings on the club's property should be well maintained and the committee will have responsibility for repairs and replacements, as well as the safety and soundness of the building structures.

It would be an advantage to encourage members who are either professional tradesmen or competent handymen (or handywomen) to become members of this committee.

The ground committee
This should consist of a member of the management committee and one member from each section which uses any outdoor facilities—pitches,

courts, lawns etc. If any club member has knowledge of the maintenance of facilities he should be encouraged to join this committee.

The main responsibilities are the care of the ground and maintenance of equipment, e.g. tractors, rollers, and making the decision,
after discussion with the groundsman (if there is one), as to whether
the ground is fit for play during adverse weather conditions.

The bar committee

This should consist of at least three members, one of whom should be
on the management committee. Paradoxically while the bar's profits
are often the main source of funding the club's activities the duties of
the bar committee are often unpopular with members. These duties
include arranging a bar rota system, ordering and checking stock on a
regular basis, negotiating with suppliers, applying for an extension of
opening hours, training volunteers who man the bar, ensuring it is an
attractive part of the social scene in the club, supervising paid employees and checking that gambling machines are correctly secured.

The social committee

This should consist of a member of the management committee,
representatives from the playing sections and anyone else who is
enthusiastic to assist.

Their responsibility is in organising the club's social activities (see
Chapter Two) so that club members are able to enjoy themselves and
funds are raised. Any social functions which regularly lose money
should be closely examined to see if they should be repeated.

Playing and coaching committee

This should be small with a member of the management committee
and one experienced player from each sporting section.

Regulations governing behaviour of playing members should be
contained in the club's overall rules. One job of this committee is
to ensure that these are being observed. A club whose players are
regularly contravening the spirit and laws of the game can soon find
itself in serious trouble. Not only will opponents begin to break off
fixtures but well behaved club members will not tolerate the situation
and possibly look for another club offering similar facilities which has
a better record.

It would be in the club's interests if any serious playing incidents
are reported to the management committee.

Many clubs now take coaching very seriously, especially if they
wish to develop the skills of their own members, especially beginners
and juniors. This committee could monitor and compare progress
which is made within the club and offer practical help to the different
sections.

1. MANAGEMENT OF A CLUB

Finance committee

This should consist of the honorary treasurer, a member from each section, a member of the bar committee, social committee and the planning committee. Its responsibilities would be to review the club's overall viability, preparing accounts for external auditing, recommending subscription levels, initiating fund raising, and in conjunction with the planning committee examine the cost implications of future developments in the club.

Although most members of this committee should be experienced in financial matters by being accountants, bank managers etc., it would prove interesting if at least one member was not experienced in this field—although many questions asked by this person may sound silly they could equally be perceptive.

Planning committee

This should consist of a member of the management committee and a representative of each sporting section. It should liaise with the finance committee.

Its brief should be to forecast both the short term (about two years) and the long term (five to ten years) development of the club. Major developments should be investigated and different options compared, for instance the implications of changing a natural playing surface to an artificial surface.

Sectional committee

Each activity conducted in a club should have its own committee with sub-committees where necessary. Members should be elected annually with co-opted members where necessary. Very often the sectional committee, while being responsible to the overall management committee, has a great deal of autonomy in its own affairs—not only within the club but in relation to outside bodies, for instance when sending delegates to county or regional governing bodies of sports meetings.

Sectional committees are the first level for discussion and they can consider many subjects in greater depth than could be afforded within the wider context of the club. If a sport is seasonal, it is during the playing time that the sectional committee should be most active.

Although these are the main committees within the club the following committees could be considered useful in certain circumstances.

Tournament committee

Many clubs organise tournaments which give prestige to the club, offer opportunities for club members to participate and allow the possibility of raising funds for the club. In view of the complexities of organising the event successfully (see Chapter Three), it may be advisable for a tournament committee to be set up, normally under overall control of one person. The size of the committee should be as small as practically possible and in view of both sexes either participating or attending it would be advisable for both sexes to be represented on the committee.

Publicity and public relations committee

This could be set up in conjunction with the management committee, one of whose members should be a member of this committee and also the social committee.

A small number of members who have experience of the media—newspapers, radio, advertising, television—could be asked to serve. Although their task is normally unlikely to be onerous there could arise incidents which affect neighbours such as cricket balls being hit into adjacent property. To avoid bad feeling and possible litigation, it is important that one member of the committee be appointed public relations officer and be responsible for trying to minimise these problems and show that the club is trying to solve the problem in as responsible a way as possible.

"Am I to assume we have a difference of opinion
on this point about hooliganism?"

Juniors committee
This would inform the management committee of the views of the junior members of the club. It will help arrange junior tournaments and social events, although senior members should be appointed in an advisory capacity. The committee could consist of a member of the management committee, a member of the coaching staff and the most responsible juniors. Juniors should be in the majority in the question of voting.

This committee shall be allocated some funds so it is able to have the means to finance its events. The appointment of a junior treasurer would both enable financial expertise to be responsibly demonstrated and groom a possible future officer of the club.

It is important that senior members who join this committee realise that the junior members, while being enthusiastic, are inexperienced and often frustration (on both sides) will be encountered. People who have experience with dealing with youngsters should be encouraged to participate. These could include teachers, housewives, coaches or social workers.

Ladies committee
The role of ladies in sports clubs varies from full participation in the club's affairs to being denied the right of participating at all in the management process. Although many women may not wish to become part of the management committee or any of the other key committees, it should be recognised that an increasing number may wish to make as full a contribution to the club's activities as possible.

Clubs which do discriminate should address themselves to this question and if they are able to offer women wider powers they should do so. It is unlikely with lower participation on average by women that they will be able to "take over" the running of a club. If women are given full rights often the price to be paid by them will be increased membership fees comparable with male members.

However, if the female part of the club's membership feel they need their own committee where their views can be aired, it is important to try to persuade them to have male representation. This will give them a link with the rest of the club's membership.

Catering committee
Although it could be said that the responsibilities of this committee and the social committee overlap, the difference in function is that whereas the social committee organises events in total—arranging the music, setting up equipment at the summer fete—the catering committee looks after the day-to-day catering facilities, organising a rota system for post-match teas, ensuring that the questions of safety and hygiene in the kitchen areas have been examined. At least one

member of the management committee and the social committee should be represented on this committee.

OFFICERS

As well as ensuring enough club members are willing to serve on various committees, clubs have to fill specialist posts which carry different levels of responsibility. The main officers are:

— chairman;
— secretary;
— treasurer;
— auditor.

The chairman

In a sports club, as in many other organisations, the chairman is one of the most influential people. His main task is to guide discussions and to ensure that business being discussed is carried through at meetings.

In meetings it is advantageous if decisions can be taken which are the general view of the members present. If necessary, however, a vote should be recorded. It is the chairman's role to try to gauge the feelings of those present and try wherever possible to avoid the subject being taken to a vote. This may prevent acrimony within the club at a later time. The chairman should abstain unless his casting vote is necessary to obtain a result. Unless members are willing for a subject to be discussed at a later time action should be taken one way or the other.

The chairman should always allow all present to give their views but must be firm in knowing when to stop a speaker from monopolising the debate. If anyone is denied the opportunity to participate then there will be grounds for possible criticism later. To this end a reticent or new member should be encouraged to participate.

Although most chairmen tend to be older and experienced, if a suitable younger member of the club wishes to take on the job, and understands the responsibility it entails, he should be encouraged to do so. A good idea is for a club or section of club to have two vice-chairmen, one of whom must be under a certain age, e.g. under 30.

The club secretary

He will probably be the official with most administrative work to do. His duties will be wide ranging from arranging meetings, notifying those who have to be present and taking minutes, to answering correspondence and applying for a registration certificate, for the sale and supply of alcohol under the Licensing Act, 1964.

1. MANAGEMENT OF A CLUB

It is important for the club to ensure that the secretary is a trust-worthy and responsible person who is willing to undertake all his tasks. The person wishing to take up the post must realise that it will take up a great deal of his spare time, possibly infringe on his enjoyment of the club's facilities and render him liable to prosecution, for the infringement by the club of the Licensing Acts if he is the named licensee.

Because of the need for the secretary to appear impartial during a meeting he should not be able to vote on any matters and only offer guidance to members during discussions. It is advisable that he liaises very closely with the chairman of a committee, especially in the production of the meeting's agenda.

Any possible contentious items should be discussed early with the more routine subjects following later, for most members will have been working during the day and will become tired during evening meetings and have less concentration as the meeting progresses.

Clear communication between the secretary and club members and those dealing with the club is vital. The secretary should keep written records of any verbal instructions he may give; this may reduce confusion at a later date. A book or diary listing details of availability, or not, of club facilities should be available in the clubhouse by the secretary—to avoid overbooking and to answer telephone enquiries.

Although most clubs will find a suitable volunteer for this post from within the membership they should consider paid or unpaid assistance from outside. Wives of members may be able to offer skills, such as typing or minute taking, which may lead them to be ideal candidates. The club should vote on the amount of money to be used as expenses by the secretary e.g. on postage, telephone calls. All expenses should be accountable to the treasurer. However, if a small amount of money is made available as an honorarium or salary, this may be appreciated by the incumbent in the post.

The club treasurer

He should be a member of the overall management committee and also act as chairman of the finance committee. His main attribute shall be complete honesty. He should be one of the authorised signatories of cheques drawn on the club's current account and will need to be satisfied that any expenditure made by the club is legitimate.

If he is not satisfied he should confer as soon as possible with the appropriate person in authority who has incurred the expense on the club's behalf. The treasurer should also familiarise himself with the methods of raising revenue and here he should liaise with the bar committee and subscriptions secretary.

The treasurer in conjunction with the finance committee should draw up a statement of account at regular intervals as this can be used for a variety of reasons e.g. forecasting cash flow problems, assisting in grant applications. It will also make preparation of the annual income and expenditure accounts and balance sheet easier.

It is preferable that the treasurer have some experience of financial affairs and the most suitable candidate should come from this field. However, many of the club's financial affairs are quite simple and numeracy and commonsense would be the chief attributes for treasurer.

The club auditor

He should be a qualified professional, preferably an accountant who will look at the club's financial affairs in an impartial and searching way. If this task is done by a non-member the club should realise that a fee will be charged for this service and provision made in the club's budget accordingly. It may be possible to minimise this in different ways—for example, by offering the work to a firm for whom a club member works, who for goodwill will often reduce their fee or offer a reduction if other work is given to the auditing company. In many cases the auditor will be from within the club's membership. It is essential that members and especially the treasurer offer as much co-operation to the auditor as possible.

A word of warning—not only is the club audited but the treasurer is audited also.

Other jobs that may be allotted are publicity officer, club captain and membership secretary.

The publicity officer

He should be a member of the publicity and public relations committee and would be responsible, using guidelines laid down by the committee, for contacting the media. He should ensure that notices are issued concerning pre-season training with regard to recruiting new players or submitting match reports for weekly publication by the local newspaper. The advantage of having one person delegated to do these tasks is that there becomes a continuity in liaison and personal contacts are made. It would be of help to the publicity officer if he had an assistant with whom he could share the workload. Not only would this lighten his duties but the assistant could be groomed to take over if the officer became unable to carry out his job for whatever reason, or if he resigned from the post. Because it is important for the two to work as a team, the publicity officer should be able to select his assistant without requiring prior permission from the committee. If the committee is unhappy with the choice they can express their views.

The club captain

This is a job which is hard to define. In some sports such as golf or sailing the club captain is expected to carry out many duties. In other cases the club captain is often regarded as a figurehead with little to do.

The main requirement of the club captain is to be able to discuss club affairs with members in a tactful way, often explaining how and why certain decisions have been reached. It is advisable for the club captain to have a standing invitation to meetings of the management committee as an observer with no voting rights. If a club has several sections with their own captains to invite them all would make the system unwieldy and impractical. The secretary should invite for discussion only those captains whose sections are immediately affected.

It is important that a club captain be approachable by members because they may not feel able to broach a subject direct with a member of the committee. He should be an experienced member of the club and preferably someone with a good playing record. The club captain should welcome new members to the club and after a short period ensure they have settled in; it is at this time that any misgivings may be voiced. The club captain could be asked first if he would like to represent the club at any outside functions, such as tournaments or other clubs' annual dinners.

The membership secretary
He is one of the members of the financial team together with the treasurer and auditor. It will be shown in Chapter Two that subscriptions are one of the main sources of club revenue and are a normally predictable way of assisting the club's activities. He should be advised by the secretary, or another club official, when a new player has been accepted for membership and together with the secretary deal with any queries from prospective members.

It is important that accurate membership records are maintained as these can be used for circulation purposes and for requirements under licensing laws. These can be produced in a variety of ways from a simple sheet which is updated at regular intervals, to a computerised system with a software programme which can be used for analysis for planning purposes—geographical location of members, members' ages, occupations etc.

The membership secretary has to be firm when it comes to the question of paying subscriptions. It should be explained to members why subscriptions are due at a certain time and the problem for the club's cash liquidity which is caused by any delay. It is the job of the membership secretary to inform the different sporting sections' committee if any subscription is unpaid by the time due. If the player has not paid by that time his attention should be drawn to the fact and he should be informed that he will not be allowed to continue playing without paying his dues. As a final resort it may be necessary for the matter to be referred to the management committee. If this can be prevented it will save unnecessary embarrassment.

It is helpful for the membership secretary if the club's rules allow a reduction if subscriptions are paid early. This is the carrot to counter-act the stick of preventing a member participating for non or late payment. If there are several sections in a club, it may be advisable for each of them to have their own membership secretary. These could meet occasionally to discuss their methods and compare notes.

TYPES OF SPORTS CLUBS

There are different methods by which clubs can be formed and then run. It is the needs of the club's members and the purpose for which the club was formed which will determine how this is done. Clubs and their committees should bear in mind, however, that their constitution can be altered if this will help the club's situation and allow them to take advantage of financial benefits which may become available. If a club has been in existence successfully for many years any fundamental changes should be viewed with great caution.

The majority of sports clubs are voluntary associations which do not exist as a legal entity unless they become incorporated under the Companies Acts, or are granted a Royal Charter or become a proprietary club. The different types of club have different features. The categories of club are as follows:

1. Members' (non-profit distributing) clubs. Any profits which are made from the club's operation are used for the members' benefit. Only on winding up may any assets be distributed after liabilities have been met.
2. Members' (non-profit distributing) clubs with trustees.
3. Clubs as limited companies:
   — limited by share issue;
   — limited by guarantee and not having a share issue.
4. Clubs which operate partly as a company and partly as a members' club.
5. Proprietary clubs.
6. Clubs with charitable status.
7. Clubs which register as a Friendly Society under the Friendly Societies Act, 1974.
8. Clubs which register under the Industrial and Provident Societies Acts, 1965 and 1968.

Members' clubs
These do not have a legal existence of their own and as such cannot sue or be sued nor prosecuted in their own name but only through

their officers. The rules of the club show how it is constituted and how the members' association with each other is set out. While outsi le organisations such as brewers, banks, insurance companies etc. would be willing to deal with officials, it is likely that the ownership and management of items with high value such as land, buildings and major items of equipment will necessitate a more formalised system. This system is embodied by the appointment of trustees.

Members' clubs with trustees

If trustees are appointed by a club this procedure will overcome the problems associated with major items such as the ownership and management of land and the holding of investments. Although a bank may be willing to act as trustee for a club, this option will probably have the disadvantage of both costing the club money and also taking control of the club's affairs slightly away from the club. It would be better for willing individuals who are associated with the club to act as trustees. A solicitor should be employed to draw up a trust deed which will appoint the first trustees (at least three) and lay down the method of replacing them. An odd number of trustees will ensure any votes have a result. A clause in the deed should be included which will state that they act with the wishes of the management committee and in the best interests of the club. The assets of the club must be held on behalf of and for the benefit of the club, and trustees must not be able to dispose of the assets without the agreement of club members.

Clubs as limited companies

If clubs want to obtain corporate status to enable them to issue debentures or more importantly limit the liability of officers, committee and members, this can be achieved by registration under the Companies Acts either by:

1. forming themselves as a company limited by shares; or
2. becoming a company limited by guarantee and not having a share capital.

Before a club begins to take up either of these options it should discuss the implications with an accountant or solicitor as they are normally designed for use by commercial ventures and there are obligations contained in the various Companies Acts. Although the initial cost of forming a company can be quite low (approximately £100 to £150), if standard provisions need re-drafting the costs can soon escalate.

Company limited by shares

Members can take advantage of any profits the club's activities may make. If the club should cease trading, individual shareholders' liability is limited to the value of the share which is held. This is the biggest difference to a member club where any financial liability is borne by the members, the committee or appointed trustees.

If the club allows members or shareholders to receive any profit or dividend during its existence or on dissolution, this may disqualify the club from receiving financial assistance in the way of loans, grants or rate relief from central or local government and national agencies such as the Sports Council.

The club's financial statement should be lodged at Companies House and this can be examined by members of the public. Administrative problems are caused when a member dies or resigns from a club.

Company limited by guarantee and not having a share capital

Members' liability is limited to the sum guaranteed by them. The club (company) does not have shareholders and as no shares are issued consequently no profits can be distributed. This type of organisation is able to fulfil the requirements laid down to enable them to receive financial assistance from central and local government and their agencies.

An incorporated club adopting either system has to have a Memorandum which contains the objects of the club and Articles of Association which contain the rules and show how the objectives will be met. These legal documents lay down the form of the company and should be drawn up by a solicitor.

Members' clubs combined with a limited company

Sometimes when a club has a large amount of assets in the form of buildings, land or equipment and its activities involve a large number of financial transactions, it may be preferable for a limited company to be formed to handle these by the parent members' club which will deal with routine matters.

It is important that when the subsidiary limited company is set up, it is made clear that club members have control of the running of the limited company and that any profits or dividends are used for the benefit of members.

Proprietary club

Proprietary clubs are normally run on a commercial basis with the owner or proprietor taking any profits or sustaining any losses. Although there may be a members' committee which will represent members who pay their subscription in the normal way, the ultimate control of the club, especially in financial matters, lies in the hands of the proprietor. The members will be bound by the club's rules but they will have no financial liability.

1. MANAGEMENT OF A CLUB

Industrial sports clubs

Often a club will be set up as a business house club and may be heavily subsidised with any operating profits being re-invested in the club's facilities. This type of club is similar to an ordinary voluntary club. Increasingly this type of club is coming under threat of closure as businesses examine the use of their assets. Members should be aware of the firm's situation and if possible try to take over its assets if it is put up for sale.

Clubs with charitable status

Although sport as an activity in itself is not legally recognised as being charitable as such, there are many voluntary organisations which are charitable and organise sporting activities. These include the YMCA and many playing fields associations.

If an organisation achieves charitable status it immediately derives many benefits. In the financial field, these include:

1. A mandatory 50 per cent rate relief which is allowable under Section 40(1) of the General Rate Act 1967 and also a possible discretionary rate relief which can be offered under Section 40(5) of the same legislation.
2. Benefit from tax rebates from covenants which are made by income tax payers for a period of more than four or seven years.
3. Exemption from investment tax and capital transfer tax.
4. The possibility of organising a local door-to-door collection to raise funds.
5. The ability to set up subsidiary trading organisations whose profits can be covenanted back to the charity.

If all these benefits can accrue to a charity why is it that all clubs do not try for this status? The main reason is that membership of charitable clubs should be open to all members of the community and that the club committee would not be able to approve candidates for membership.

Also all members shall be represented on the committee through their sectional interest. There is no way that a certain section could be denied representation. If the club was dissolved, no assets could be distributed to club members. Any assets remaining after liabilities have been met would have to be transferred to another charitable organisation having objects similar to those of the charity.

If a club wishes to register as a charity under the Charities Act 1960 with the Charity Commission the categories which are available for charitable status are:

1. MANAGEMENT OF A CLUB

— the relief of poverty;
— the advancement of religion;
— the advancement of education;
— other purposes beneficial to the community.

The other charitable legislation which is applicable to sports clubs is the Recreational Charities Act 1958.

The club must apply for registration to the Charity Commissioners whose addresses are given in Appendix E. It is necessary to submit a copy of the draft, or existing constitution/rules, of the organisation, or alternatively the Articles of Association and form of Memorandum, setting out the aims (called objects) and how those will be achieved (called the powers) such as membership qualifications, committee structure and how financial affairs will be managed. Once the constitution has been agreed, two copies of the adopted constitution and application form should be sent to the Commission.

The Commission will then submit the application to the Inland Revenue at Bootle who will consider the charity's eligibility for financial purposes as listed above. If both bodies are satisfied with an application and a charitable registration number is given to an organisation, then the organisation can start to use its new status. Depending on factors such as holidays, current applications, number of applications etc., the application could be finalised within three months.

It is important that an application is submitted correctly in the first instance and although the expense of employing a specialist solicitor to make the application may be high (possibly £1,500 plus) the benefit of achieving this status quickly will help offset the expense.

The best type of solicitor to be approached is one experienced with charity formation. A list of these is produced by the Law Society, and can be seen at the Citizens Advice Bureau and local library. The solicitor should be asked to give an estimate of cost (hourly rate), the time scale involved and what priority the application will be given. It is useful for an organisation thinking of applying for charitable status to look at the constitutions of accepted organisations with similar aims, e.g. the promotion of recreation. This can be done by looking at the register of charities which is kept at the Central Register of Charities, the address of which is given in Appendix E. There is no charge for this service and the register contains a contact for the relevant charities.

The advancement of education through the provision of sports facilities is charitable and a club if it is coaching youngsters could use and register this part of its activities exclusively to qualify for charitable status if the rest of its activities are not charitable. A saving could be made on rates for any part of property used for this purpose.

1. MANAGEMENT OF A CLUB

The Recreational Charities Act 1958 was intended to make it clear that it is charitable to provide or assist in the provision of facilities for recreation and other leisure time occupations if the facilities are provided in the interest of social welfare. A charity must benefit the whole community and membership should not be used as a restriction, only a geographical basis is considered.

A Memorandum which should be acceptable for all charitable purposes is:

"The object of the Association shall be the provision in the interest of social welfare of facilities for recreation and other leisure time occupations for the inhabitants of ...... being facilities

(a) of which those persons have need by reason of their youth, age, infirmity or disablement, poverty or social and economic circumstances and;

(b) which will improve the conditions of life for such persons by promoting their physical, mental or spiritual well-being."

A club can show that deprivation can exist by showing that the club's facilities do not exist locally. It is important for the terms of a constitution not to be too narrow because it is easier to start big at first than try to alter rules at a later date.

Finally if the Charity Commissioners do not immediately accept an application—*persevere*, amendments or modifications can always be resubmitted.

There is no cost to an applicant for registration and it is possible to obtain some informal advice from the Charity Commission. If an organisation contains different sports sections these can each have their own rules separate from one another which should not conflict with the spirit of the charity. If a charity is in existence, small alterations do have to be sent for approval but important changes do not have to be approved; in any event Inland Revenue surveillance points towards confirmation for all developments.

Clubs registered under the Friendly and Industrial and Provident Societies Acts

Voluntary clubs can be registered under the Friendly Societies Act 1974 or the Industrial and Provident Societies Acts 1965 and 1968. To date, only a relatively small number have taken advantage of these options (for instance in 1982 only 3,683 social and recreational clubs had registered under the Industrial and Provident Societies Acts).

Registration is administered by the Chief Registrar of Friendly Societies who is employed by the minister for the civil service.

1. MANAGEMENT OF A CLUB

Organisations registered under the Friendly Societies Act 1974.
Different types of societies can be registered under this Act.
These can range from Working Men's Clubs who can register under
Section 7(1)(d), to charitable societies who can register under Section
7(1)(e).

There is a scale of fees for registration and that for a new society at
present is £220. Although the provisions of the legislation are varied
some of the most important points are:

— every registered society shall have one or more trustees;
— qualified auditors shall be appointed in most cases;
— annual returns should be submitted to the Registrar;
— members shall have the right to inspect the society's books;
— legal sanctions can be brought if legal requirements are not met.

***Organisations registered under the Industrial and Provident
Societies Acts 1965 and 1968.*** Non-profit distributing sports clubs can
be registered under these Acts. The club's rules must show that assets
will not be distributed among its members; it must have at least seven
members; the proposed name of a society is not undesirable; and that
all matters required by Schedule 1 of the Act have been satisfied.

While it is possible that clubs may wish to use "model rules" which
have been prepared by certain approved "promoting bodies", it is
more likely that the club will have its own rules, either in draft or
substantive form. A club may be advised to obtain a list of these
"promoting bodies" which is available from the Registrar on demand.
If an application using a model rule is submitted, it must be made
through and endorsed by the secretary of the body concerned. At
present the cost of registering a new society is £300. The requirements
of the Acts are similar to those of the Friendly Societies Act.

On balance it would seem to be preferable for a voluntary club
wishing to register under these Acts to choose to be registered under
the Industrial and Provident Societies Act as their provisions are more
appropriate. The advantages of this Act are:

— that they ensure members' liability is limited with a corporate
  status being adopted;
— rules and objects are clearly defined;
— members' share capital can be easily withdrawn.

In reality there are few filing or registration controls, although the
accounts of clubs are clearly monitored with legal penalties being
available for dishonesty.

The Registrar of Friendly Societies, whose address is given in
Appendix E, will be pleased to give informal advice at the early stages
of registration. Applicants would be advised to obtain forms F617 and

F339 which deal with registration and termination of Societies under the Industrial and Provident Societies Act 1965, and forms F822 and F823 which give the scale of fees payable for registration under this Act and the Friendly Societies Act 1974.

Summary
Management of a Club

1. **The club's structure and purpose**
   There are different types of sports club serving different groups
   with different needs. Clubs have factors which influence their
   development:
   rules;
   management style;
   meetings;
   committees and officers.

2. **The club rules**
   There are essential rules which have to be applied, e.g. aims,
   election of new members and committee members, rule changes.
   There are other rules which can be set out but which are not so
   important, e.g. club colours, behaviour byelaws.

3. **The management style**
   Factors which help determine the atmosphere within a club, e.g.
   communications within the club, approach to members by
   officials.

4. **Meetings**
   To be successful meetings need the following;
   planning—plenty of notice, appropriate timing i.e. during
              the playing season, the correct venue;
   conduct —good chairman and secretary, agenda followed,
              main points of view put, voting correctly
              conducted, decisions known.

5. **Committees**
   Although fourteen different committees are identified and
   described, the size, style, aims and facilities of clubs will vary
   and consequently the number of committees will vary. To be
   kept under review if circumstances change. Normally, the
   smaller the club the lower the number of committees needed.

6. Officers

The role and qualities of the main officers—chairman, secretary, treasurer and auditor are discussed.

Other officers in the club—publicity officer, captain and membership secretary are examined together with their relation to members and other officials.

---

7. Types of sports club

The different forms that a voluntary sports club can take, e.g. members' club, members' club with trustees, charitable status, limited companies etc. are discussed. When a club is formed with few assets it may wish to be a simple members' club and then evolve as it grows and adopt a more appropriate form of existence. Circumstances will vary.

2
Financial Aspects of a Club

"Annual income twenty pounds, annual expenditure nineteen pounds nineteen and six, result happiness. Annual income twenty pounds, annual expenditure twenty pounds ought and six, result misery."

Although Mr Micawber's words are taken from fiction, their sound economic sense applies to sports clubs, especially those of a voluntary nature, as much as to individuals and other types of organisation.

FINANCIAL PLANNING PRINCIPLES

The sports club normally has to make its books balance at the very least to allow it to carry out its activities which are designed to meet a varied number of needs.

Although it is the primary responsibility of the club officers who are responsible for financial matters, such as the treasurer and membership secretary, to have an awareness of the need to maximise income and minimise costs, there is also a general duty on *all* club members to be aware of and try to fulfil this simple philosophy.

The club's financial methods are normally designed to:

1. Raise finance to allow current activities to take place and ensure that facilities and equipment are maintained.
2. Assist short term planning, especially the development of policies to meet anticipated expenditure.
3. Help the introduction of new major (or capital) projects, e.g. clubhouse, courts which will develop new activities.
4. Assist long term planning so that the club's progress can be carried out in a measured way with alternative projects receiving due consideration.

The issues raised in reasons 1 and 2 will be examined in this chapter and reasons 3 and 4 will be contained in Chapter Three. As some of these aims overlap—for instance the installation of a capital or large scale project in the long term will have an effect on day-to-day running costs when it is introduced—the two chapters should be read in conjunction.

2. FINANCIAL ASPECTS OF A CLUB

SHORT TERM PLANNING

Although club officers often suffer from lack of time to carry out as detailed an analysis as they would like to improve the club's financial situation, there are certain recurring items which are common to most clubs and which feature in their annual statement of accounts and balance sheets.

It is hoped that the glossary of financial terms which is included in Appendix B will be of use to those not greatly experienced in the world of finance and will help in examining and discussing financial affairs, either within the club or with external contacts such as suppliers or grant-aiding bodies.

Recurrent financial topics can be best categorised under two headings which are:

Income
Expenditure

INCOME

Income can be derived from the following sources:

1. subscriptions (including joining fees);
2. bar receipts;
3. receipts from food sales;
4. revenue from machines of different types;
5. match fees;
6. assistance from local authorities;
7. prize money;
8. sale of goods;
9. hire of club facilities;
10. donations, sponsorships and advertising;
11. interest from investment;
12. regular social events.

Subscriptions

Duration. Subscriptions are normally levied annually. But there should also be provision for monthly, quarterly, weekly, daily rates which would be attractive, for instance, to visitors on holiday who may wish to use indoor facilities if the weather is bad, or to students or businessmen who may be locally resident for short periods.

Categories. The following categories of membership could be introduced within the club:

— full;
— off peak;
— weekend;
— weekday;
— junior;
— senior;
— social non-playing;
— county;
— patrons, presidents or vice-presidents;
— ladies;
— honorary;
— sectional;
— overseas;
— life;
— student;
— ex-playing;
— corporate.

No doubt many clubs will have a membership category which is similar to those shown above but which is known by a different title. No matter, the important thing is that all applicants are catered for in some way.

It is difficult to lay down hard and fast rules about the eligibility of members' suitability for each category. The two principles to be followed are firstly, that the correct category of membership meets the needs of the individual, and secondly the maximisation of revenue to the club.

Although full membership enables both parties—the club and the member—to benefit to the full, there are often instances where the membership of a certain section should be encouraged. This situation should be encouraged for instance when a facility is being under-utilised, e.g. off-peak bookings are not meeting expectations or certain user groups such as juniors or senior members are not available in sufficient numbers. If full membership is complete, there should be other categories available which will encourage people to participate in a club's affairs and not be deterred. They could be offered off-peak or weekday membership and then be put onto a waiting list with preference over those who do not take up this option. By doing this, the club benefits by having its facilities used at unfavoured times. The member benefits from receiving preferential treatment and also by meeting the club's members. If there is a membership waiting list, it is helpful for aspiring members to be informed at regular intervals about the membership situation, i.e. their position on the list and the length of time anticipated before they can join the club.

"Maybe we could change to skiing?"

The waiting list should be adhered to firmly and no queue jumping should be tolerated unless there are exceptional reasons such as when a local influential politician expresses an interest—the old adage of 'it's not what you know but who you know' holds true even for sports clubs. Other people who should be encouraged include prominent industrialists, financial leaders and celebrities.

Subscription rates. One of the most difficult financial questions to be answered in a voluntary club is at what rate to set subscriptions. The main aim of subscriptions, which is often forgotten, is to maximise revenue while at the same time not dissuading people from becoming or remaining members. When subscription rates are being set the following factors should be considered:

1. The quality and quantity of facilities being offered to club members.
2. The level of subscriptions and facilities at other similar clubs in the area, and the rates being charged by alternative providers of similar facilities, e.g. at local authority or commercial sports centres.
3. Whether the subscription rate is designed to be at a low level with high match/playing fees or is there to be a high subscription with low or no match fee.
4. Is the subscription rate pitched at one uniform level in a multi-sport club which will allow any playing member to play any sport which is available, or is there a different rate for different sports with an entry fee being a requisite before individual sport subscriptions are levied.

36

5. Whether subscription revenue is seen as being one of the main sources of fund raising for an identifiable project.
6. If financial assistance is to be sought from outside sources it is likely that they will ask for the club to charge members a reasonable subscription. If subscriptions are too high they may be viewed as eliminating certain members of the public from being able to join. If the rate is too low the club is unlikely to be able to finance its share of any additional cost attached to new large facilities.

Whenever these factors are used in the calculation of future subscription rates, it is important for as much information about other sport clubs to be obtained as possible. If there is an adverse reaction from members of other clubs to high subscriptions with low match fees, this could be mirrored in one's own club.

Although a finance or planning committee should recommend the level of subscription to the general club management committee, the decision to ratify the rates to be charged should be agreed by the club members at the club's annual general meeting. The club's rules should specify that a decision on the subscription level must be taken at this meeting. This will safeguard against the matter not being resolved and passed back for future discussion with future planning and cash flow being consequently disrupted.

Members should be given as much information as possible before the annual general meeting with copies of relevant information, e.g. treasurer's report, accounts and balance sheet with projected costs. At the meeting the treasurer or other officer should be prepared to defend the proposed subscription rate. The chairman of the meeting should be careful to control discussion on this matter and ensure that a decision is arrived at. If there are any objectors to the committee's recommended rates they could be asked to propose, on the spot, alternative levels and these could be debated. It is not likely that this alternative will be accepted as not as much thought can be put into this complex subject at an AGM as the committee can give to it.

Once agreed, the different subscription rates should be clearly displayed in the clubhouse, in the club handbook, on application forms and if possible mentioned in any club newsletter.

If the club wants to encourage *family membership* there should be incentives for this to be taken up. For instance, a husband and wife subscription should not be as high as two individual memberships. Similarly, if *junior membership* is being offered this should be at a lower rate than senior membership. It is not likely that juniors will be able to avail themselves of all the club's facilities, such as the bar or licensed entertainment, so it would not be fair to charge them as much as adults. Also many clubs should see their junior members as the lifeblood for the future, especially if they do not attract many members from outside.

Life membership may be attractive to members who feel settled at the club. If the rate is set too low there will be a loss of revenue in a few years time if too many members take advantage of it.

Social membership should be seen as an additional way of raising revenue from people who will not wear out the playing facilities. It is likely that some social members will want to take up an activity after they have experienced the club's atmosphere. The club should ensure that social membership is not a method of queue jumping if there is a waiting list, e.g. to join a squash section, and priority is given to members of any category over playing members or potential members from outside.

Corporate membership can be especially valuable in forging links between the club and outside organisations and in the generation of income at off-peak periods and in the social area—catering and the bar. Care must be taken in negotiations with outside bodies, normally industrial or commercial firms and if the experience to handle negotiations is not present within the club an outside body such as the Sports Council could be approached for informal advice.

Subscriptions as part of a club's income. The revenue from subscriptions can be forecast quite accurately from past years and as a rough guide a club's income can be apportioned as follows:

$33\frac{1}{3}$% subscriptions;
$33\frac{1}{3}$% bar (if a club has one);
$33\frac{1}{3}$% other sources.

Payment methods. There are various ways by which subscriptions can be paid and the possession by a club of a current bank account increases the number of options open to members. The methods available are:

— cash;
— cheque or postal order;
— direct debit or standing order;
— credit card e.g. Visa, Access, American Express.
  Note: Visa and Barclaycard will charge a joining fee of approximately £40 and a percentage of receipts for their facilities. For full details a club should contact their regional office.

Members can be asked to pay either annually or by instalments. If the latter method is used a small addition to the annual rate could reasonably be charged by the club as additional paperwork will be involved.

Increasing subscription revenue by recruiting new members. Clubs should always be careful to monitor their membership situation to ensure that the maximum acceptable numbers are being accommodated.

2. FINANCIAL ASPECTS OF A CLUB

This will be one of the main duties of the membership secretary and the situation should exist whereby he gives a regular report on the numbers to the management committee. If there are different sections within the club he should ensure that an officer from each section liaises with him on this matter.

If vacancies do exist and it is decided to invite new applicants for membership there are several ways in which this can be done.

Within the club. Current members can be encouraged to widen their activities, e.g. winter sports players may like to consider playing a summer sport. They must be made aware that opportunities exist and this can be done by posters or notices in the clubhouse, by personal letter to their home, or by word of mouth.

If there are junior players they could be asked to try to recruit their parents or other relatives. All members could canvass their colleagues, friends and relatives. To assist recruitment special offers regarding fees could be offered, e.g. half rates in the first year. To encourage members' recruitment efforts, a small prize could be given to the individual who is able to introduce most new members.

Outside the club. Not all clubs have to advertise for new members; some, such as certain golf, sailing, squash and racquets and health clubs are so prestigious or offer such excellent facilities that people apply to join them and have to join a waiting list and are vetted carefully by a committee or club officials.

If a club decides to advertise, this could be organised by the membership secretary with assistance from other club officials if he requests this. Different possible methods will have different costs and it would be advisable for a budget to be set aside for this purpose. It should be stressed that presentation of the club's image is very important as the first impression of any organisation is often the lasting impression. The following options are available:

1. Posters displayed in prominent places e.g. shops, library. This may be done free or at a small cost.
2. Inserts in the local newspaper(s) sports page (usually free) or adverts in the local newspaper (for a small fee).
3. Mention on local radio, either free or for a small fee.
4. Details sent to local firms, schools and establishments of further education (including any night schools locally).
5. Notices in the magazine of the relevant sports body. This may attract players who have moved into an area and who are looking to join a club.
6. Open day at the club with demonstrations or special matches, tournaments or coaching ("try it" days); club members should be available wearing club insignia if possible to assist visitors. Special arrangements should be made concerning catering, the

bar and toilets. Precautions against inclement weather would be advisable.

7. Visiting players and supporters may also be attracted to a club if they prefer its facilities to those of their own club. Membership forms and brochures about the club should always be easily available, e.g. from the bar or the foyer. Although many will be discarded some will be utilised if attractively "packaged". The cost of printing forms and brochures normally reduces proportionately with a large print run.

Bar sales and receipts

The importance of bar takings and its levels of profitability can be seen from the accounts of clubs which have a licensed bar mainly for the sale of alcoholic drink. It could be argued that without the bar many clubs would either cease to exist or have to curtail the facilities offered to members. As well as providing a meeting place for playing members it is often also the main attraction for a club's social members. It can also be used as a facility for social events such as dances, birthday parties and meetings which may be organised by the club to raise funds and which may attract both members and non-members.

The following goods are normally sold in the bar:

— spirits;
— beers and cider;
— mixers;
— soft drinks;
— food, e.g. crisps, nuts, snacks;
— tobacco, e.g. cigarettes and cigars;
— other goods such as club ties, balls, pencils.

Profit margin. There are many factors which determine the level of profit which is obtained. While some clubs may wish to maximise net profit, i.e. gross profit less wages, others may wish to make a reasonable profit with prices being depressed to encourage members to use the bar facilities. A net profit of 30 to 35 per cent would be very respectable.

Bar management. One of the biggest problems facing a club with a licensed bar is whether it should be manned by club members, either paid or unpaid, or whether a bar steward/bar staff should be employed.

The management of a bar entails skill and many responsibilities. When the club looks at these it may become clear whether members are capable of demonstrating these. If there is any doubt about this, the employment of a steward/bar staff should be agreed even if only for a trial period.

The skills and responsibilities of bar staff include:

— the ability to work independently, often long and unsociable hours on a reliable basis;
— the care to ensure security is maintained;
— the understanding of the need for high hygiene standards;
— the possession of the personality to do the job;
— the ability to look after stock and carry out its purchasing and checking efficiently.

If the club's officials and members are confident that the above items can be coped with then the bar could be run by the members. If this course is adopted there are three main disadvantages which will have to be overcome. Firstly, if the common *rota system* is introduced this has to be administered and the question of fairness in running the bar will be brought into the open. Secondly, if members are serving behind the bar they are not buying drinks at the front of the bar and consequently profit is being lost. It is unlikely that 'serving members will spend as much money when they are on duty. Thirdly, unwittingly club members may give out larger measures than paid staff who are not so involved with the club and its members.

Employment of a bar steward. The main factor in deciding whether a steward is to be employed is his ability to increase the profitability of the bar.

To obtain a good bar steward the club must expect to pay an attractive wage with the provision of on-site accommodation being an additional inducement. If too low a salary is offered, it is likely that the steward will increase his income by fiddling the takings. It would be reasonable to offer a salary of approximately £8,000/£10,000 per annum with on-site accommodation.

How can a steward increase the bar's profitability? This can be achieved in several ways:

— the reduction of dispensed free drinks;
— the possibility of increasing revenue associated with catering operations;
— the probability that the bar will be open at more times during the week;
— reduction of losses by good stock management;
— close supervision of deliveries of stock.

Other advantages of using a bar steward are:

— the bar area is likely to become more attractive;
— bad feeling between rota and non-rota members will be reduced;

— security of club facilities will be improved if a steward lives "on-site";

— there will be less likelihood of opening hours being abused with the consequent probability of loss of licence which would be disastrous;

— standards of service and quality of drink and food are likely to be constant.

A club would be wise to consider asking the steward to lodge a *good faith bond* with them which would be repaid with interest when he left, if he left on good terms with the club. Normally the secretary or the bar committee (or one of its members) will be responsible for overseeing the activities, especially financial, of the steward.

Bar profit calculation. Whether or not a bar steward is employed it is important for the club to know the profit margins of different items and the overall profit margin of all goods sold. Having this knowledge will give the club a target to aim at and if it is not reached the causes should be closely investigated.

Using existing and past sales data future income levels can be estimated and as the bar normally generates a large amount of the club's revenue this is very important for overall revenue planning.

The following example will show how the gross profit margin percentage is calculated for different items and how this relates to the overall bar profit margin and how the expected revenue per item can be forecast.

Individual items profit margin

	Selling price	Selling price less VAT (SP multiplied by 3 then divided by 23)	Cost (ex VAT)	Profit	Gross profit (% of SP less VAT)
Bitter	75p	65.2p	37p	28.2p	43.2%
Lager	85p	73.9p	46p	27.9p	37.8%
Whisky	50p	43.5p	19p	24.5p	56.3%
Mixers	25p	21.7p	16p	5.7p	26.3%

Overall profit margin

	Gross profit (% of SP less VAT)	Cost of item as % of total bar purchases
Bitter	43.2%	40%
Lager	37.8%	30%
Whisky	56.3%	20%
Mixers	26.3%	10%
		100%

(NB: This calculation does not take into account any stock changes.)

2. FINANCIAL ASPECTS OF A CLUB

Having ascertained each item's gross profit margin and each item's percentage of total bar purchases, the total bar gross profit margin is:

$$(43.2 \times 40\%) + (37.8 \times 30\%) + (56.3 \times 20\%) + (26.3 \times 10\%)$$
$$= \quad 17.28 \quad + \quad 11.34 \quad + \quad 11.26 \quad + \quad 2.63 \quad = 42.51\%$$

Although this is a very idealised, simplified list of items the profit margin is very similar to that aimed at by public houses, i.e. 40 per cent. A figure of between 30 and 40 per cent should be satisfactory; below that alarm bells should begin to ring.

An example of how income can be forecast for a certain item is as follows:

100 kegs of bitter beer each containing 80 pints are purchased in a year.
100 kegs × 80 pints = 8,000 pints
8,000 pints at 75p

Less VAT	9.8p	(NB: VAT is 3/23 of SP)
	65.2p	

Total beer revenue should be 65.2p × 8,000 = £5,216.00 (NB: this figure excludes spillage; 1–2% could be lost).

Having calculated the estimated revenue and costs the gross profit percentage can be forecast. This figure for all items on sales can be used as a control. The stock taking procedures will see if the target figure is being reached.

The regularity of stock-taking will depend on size of turnover; a weekly check will monitor the bar most effectively but monthly or quarterly checks may be sufficient. The check should be carried out by at least two individuals authorised by the bar committee or management committee or by outside auditors. The possibility of "spot" checks is of great relevance.

Low gross profit margins. There can be several reasons why the gross profit margin is not as high as expected. These can include:

— costs which have occurred have not been passed on quickly enough;
— club members' drinking habits have changed so that drinks or sundries with low profit margin have superseded those with high profit levels;
— stock-taking has not been carried out accurately;
— spillage and credits given by a brewery or supplier for returned beers, sundries has not been taken into account;
— stock has been stolen, the steward has been selling "his" unofficial drinks instead of official stock or "free" drinks have been dispensed;

43

— the playing or social programme has been unexpectedly curtailed so that sales are reduced.

Bar stocks. Like most other organisations which trade a sports club should hold as little stock as possible. The reason for this is that stock ties up cash which could earn interest in a deposit account. The secret is to know how much stock will satisfy demand, especially as there is a natural time lag between placing the order and receiving a delivery. Stock cards should be maintained and these will show the past consumption rates which can be used to predict future demand. They can also be used for stock-taking purposes.

All items should be recorded both to reduce the cash held as stocks and also to ensure that stock, especially foodstuffs, are used before it becomes inadvisable to use it on health grounds. The sale of stale crisps will not be welcomed by customers.

The layout of the bar will be mentioned in Chapter Four and the laws relating to the bar will be discussed in Chapter Five.

Bar snacks. Bar snacks should be presented in an attractive way. Meals could include chicken in the basket, burgers, pasta dishes, but the menu should not be too extensive. Clubs should recognise the growing demand for health foods and cater for this by selling lines with low sugar, salt or fat content.

Receipts from catering
A sports club is faced with several choices concerning the organisation of a catering operation and these include:

— catering carried out by club members;
— catering carried out by employees;
— catering carried out by outside organisations;
— catering carried out by a mix of the above choices.

Whichever is chosen there will be disadvantages as well as advantages.

Catering carried out by club members.
Advantages

1. Costs will be kept to a minimum mainly through the minimisation of labour costs.
2. An informal atmosphere will be engendered because everyone at a function will have the club's good at heart.

Disadvantages

1. It will be difficult for any complaint to be made directly to the members who are doing the catering.

2. It is likely that all the work will be shouldered by a few individuals and this may become a bone of contention.
3. Inexperience may be costly e.g. by over-ordering or equipment not being used properly.

Catering carried out by club employees.
Advantages

1. Standards should be professionally constant and club members will know what to expect.
2. The employees will be accountable to the club's management committee for their performance.
3. Members will not have to carry out any work.

Disadvantages

1. Costs will be increased because of the labour element and prices are therefore likely to be higher.
2. It is unlikely that employees will be as flexible as club members.
3. Any profits which are made are likely to be paid to the employees as part of their contract and not given to the club.

Catering carried out by an outside organisation.
Advantages

1. Club members will not have to do any of the work.
2. Employees do not have to be paid.
3. Quotations can be given by different organisations to cater at the club. Costs are likely to be reduced because of this factor.

Disadvantages

1. Unless the appointed caterer is reliable the club may lose control over the catering at a major function.
2. Costs may be higher due to staff involved and extraneous overheads which the firm may have to meet from "off-site" operations.

Catering carried out by a mix of groups e.g. members and outside firms
Advantages

1. Club members are able to deal with small functions, such as team teas, small meetings, thereby keeping costs down.
2. Outside organisations could be brought in for larger functions which are beyond the scope of club memebers.

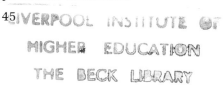

2. FINANCIAL ASPECTS OF A CLUB

Disadvantage
It is difficult to define at what level outside caterers have to be brought in.

Types of catering. The variety of catering which can be found in clubs is very great. The following types are available:

— simple bar snacks—crisps, nuts, sweets, chocolate bars;
— bar meals—chicken, scampi in a basket;
— hot and cold team meals—sandwiches, pie and beans, salads;
— restaurant meals.

The catering needs will vary within the club at different times; the playing sides will require a simple but filling meal after their matches, the annual dinner may require an elaborate multi-course meal and a disco will lend itself to a buffet style meal.

Profitability of catering. While all catering should aim to make a profit, the level of profit will vary from event to event. Probably the highest profit per head should be aimed for at events which attract outside users, for instance when the club's facilities are used for wedding receptions, birthday parties.

Strict control of portion size and cost will assist the level of profitability achieved. Bulk buying with the storage of food in freezers can also assist in reducing portion cost. Microwave cookers are a useful addition to profitability. The two cardinal rules for catering within the club are:

1. Value for money should be given. If customers, whether they are club members or outsiders, are satisfied with their treatment they will return again and hopefully bring along other people.
2. The club's catering facilities should be used to their fullest extent; this will reduce unit costs, give best return on investment of kitchen equipment (see Chapter Four for more details) and most importantly, generate income in other fields such as the fruit machines or bar. Receipts from the catering operation should be kept separate from other sources of income to assist accounting procedures.

Revenue from machines (excluding weight training equipment)
There are several types of machines which can be installed within a clubhouse which should give additional income. These are:

— gaming machines issuing prizes, e.g. "one armed bandit";
— machines which are games of skill such as pool tables;
— video games;
— vending machines which dispense goods for payment;

46

2. FINANCIAL ASPECTS OF A CLUB

— lockers which retain inserted money;
— health and weight information.

Gaming machines.

Gaming machine legislation. The installation and regulation of gaming machines which give prizes is governed by the provisions of the 1968 Gaming Act which we will look at in Chapter Five.

Financial implications. The attraction of these machines is that they can give a club a large income. Obviously the income generated will be influenced by many factors the most important of which is the usage of the machine by members. An indication of what can be achieved: two machines in a northern sports club with a membership of about 1,000 make £6,000 profit.

Most private sports clubs are allowed to use up to two machines at one time and when these machines offer one "go" for a 10p stake an annual duty payment of £750 in advance is required. This is the most popular type of machine with members as it gives the biggest jackpot. If the machine gives two goes for 10p the rate will be £300 per machine again up to a maximum of two and again *in advance*. There are lesser rates of duty payable if machines have a lower stake amount. These rates of duty are altered periodically. In addition, the licensing authority will issue a licence for £50 for five years. It is useful to know that a machine can be kept in reserve to be installed in case either machine breaks down, but only in this circumstance. If a club uses all three at one time this is illegal and the penalties can be severe. A club should only contemplate three machines if the takings from members will be severely hit if one machine goes out of action and repairs may be delayed.

A good machine will cost about £1,200. Buying carries a risk that the machine will need much maintenance, could be superseded by new models and may not remain acceptable to members; in all these cases takings will be reduced gradually.

It is preferable for a club to rent their machine(s) at a cost of £25–£35 per week per machine. For this the club should gain prompt service and normally a machine will be replaced if it is superseded or becomes unpopular.

The machine should be supplied and serviced by a bona fide operator who is certificated by the Gaming Board under the Gaming Act 1968. Although large concerns can offer a service it would be better to use a smaller, independent operator. Often all transactions will be conducted verbally and the club is in a strong position in negotiations as many suppliers will be after their business. Normally all insurance on these machines or on any other machines installed—whether bought, rented or leased—will be the responsibility of the club and not the supplier.

An additional source of information about most suppliers can be gained from the British Amusement, Catering Trades Association (BACTA) whose address is given in Appendix E.

Machines incorporating games of skill. With the recent rise in popularity in snooker and pool many clubs have installed tables on which these games can be played. A small fee is normally charged per game often on a time basis. Normally as long as they are installed correctly with correct levels being achieved to allow the balls to roll properly, there will be little in the way of running costs. Certainly, maintenance costs can be included in the contract. If a pool or snooker table is hired the cost will be in the region of £10–£15 per week with profits being shared between the club and the supplier.

It is likely that after an initial period of use interest may fall off. If this happens a club should encourage competitions between members and with other clubs to generate income. The formation of a new section would be another possibility.

Video machines. Play again machines which today are typified by computerised games, e.g. Space Invaders, Pac-Man etc., have been in the past a good source of revenue for a club. A coin or token is inserted and if a target score is reached the player receives another go, or the return of the token or coin inserted. There is no restriction on the number of machines the club is able to install and they are particularly popular with junior members.

Clubs should realise that the fashions change and these machines may have to be frequently traded in to meet demand. The siting of these machines is important for they should be positioned where they can be observed with ease by the main bulk of members to reduce the possibility of damage and theft.

Again to avoid tying up funds the machines should be rented with profit being shared with the supplier.

Vending machines. A wide range of goods and services can be offered to members from a machine. These include:

— hot and cold non-alcoholic drinks;
— snack foods, sweets and chocolates;
— sports goods, e.g. squash balls;
— cigarettes and tobacco;
— changing room lockers from which the club retains the deposit fee;
— health and weight information.

Although machine suppliers' details can be found in local Yellow Pages or from professional leisure magazines, such as the Sports

Council's *Sport and Leisure* or the *Institute of Leisure and Amenity Management's Official Journal*, the main point to remember is to approach several suppliers to gain the best possible deal. As an example of what can be achieved, the methods employed by many local independent companies specialising in supplying tobacco and cigarette products will be examined.

Tobacco and cigarettes. In return for being the sole concessionaire to provide tobacco goods, both to the bar and in machines, a supplier will assess the site and the potential of the club and provide a suitable machine. All the profits from the machine, which is regularly serviced, will be kept by the company. Profit from tobacco sold behind the bar will be retained by the club.

The club gains by not tying up money in tobacco stocks, money which could achieve a better return in beer and spirits sales. The vending company would pay the club a percentage of turnover; as this is deemed rent for the machine it would not be liable for VAT.

A hidden benefit would be the reduction of the opportunity of pilfering as only the company would be able to open the machine. A small cost to the club would be an addition to their insurance bill for say £100 worth of tobacco in the machine. The machine company would not be able to insure the machine and its contents as it is not the keyholder of the clubhouse or pavilion where the machine would be sited. The club secretary will be relieved to know that no licence is needed for a cigarette vending machine.

A club officer must be sure that the club is receiving the percentage agreed with the supplier. To ensure this it is essential that a club officer be present when the cash box is emptied and the takings counted.

Food and drink. If foodstuffs or drinks are sold from machines it is important to keep the machines clean and the stock rotated regularly so that stale goods are not bought by members. If either of these factors are ignored members will soon lose interest and takings will diminish.

Wherever possible vending machines should be regarded as back-up to goods sold either in the bar or cooked and sold fresh. Their great advantages are that they can be sited in areas such as the changing room where members can make impulse purchases, e.g. fresh orange juice, and that they can give service at times when staff are not available, e.g. outside bar opening hours or during unsocial hours.

Because of the reliability of this type of simple vending machine it would be better for these to be purchased rather than rented. The only advantage of renting a machine is that the supplier will also fill the machine. A club may, however, be able to do this itself by using a local "cash and carry" warehouse, and if this is the case additional profit will be made.

(Courtesy the Sports Council)

A vending machine can give change as well as dispensing a variety of hot and cold drinks. It should be well situated and easily accessible. A waste bin nearby would help reduce the chance of litter being dropped in the area. Note the clock which is useful for those waiting to play matches.

Sports goods. The best types of sports goods which can be bought from a vending machine are those which are small in size and relatively low in value. Examples are squash balls, racquet grips, headbands and wristlets and scorecards and pencils. As many sizes or types of equipment as possible should be displayed, but it would be impossible to meet everyone's needs.

Lockers. Players like to know that while they are taking part in their activity their ordinary clothing is secure. This is best achieved by securing it in a locked changing room. If this is not possible lockers are the best alternative. To ensure that locker keys are not misplaced payment, normally of 10p, is made by users of lockers. This can be returned to the user. Alternatively the fee may be kept by the club when the locker is opened. It may be most acceptable to members if any money kept is used for a specific purpose and the most appropriate use may be paying for the lockers as they are very expensive. Once this aim has been achieved members should be asked whether they wish this system to continue.

As costs of lockers vary according to size, style and material, it would be advisable for a club to approach several manufacturers to compare prices.

Fitness and health products. As well as considering the introduction of machines vending health products such as soap, shampoo and personal items, clubs could benefit from the recent surge in the interest in general health and body conditioning. They could consider the installation of a weight scale and/or a heart pulse machine. Both of these machines should be used for guidance about fitness condition and should not be regarded as infallible.

The cost of a good quality *weight scale* is in the region of £450 but it can be hired for about £25–£30 per week. As the cost is now 5p each weighing a break-even point can be easily calculated. The address of the nearest suppliers of these machines will be found in the Yellow Pages under "scales and weights".

The *heart pulse* machine in which the user inserts his finger to check his pulse rate is normally installed by a local licensee of the manufacturers, Mainbridge Industries Ltd, with the takings after VAT has been deducted being split 50/50 between club and licensee. It must be correctly sited.

Match fees

If a club has a system of charging members whenever they play and use facilities, it should try to ensure that the cost of the facility is covered by the user. Very often a club will not know accurately the cost of the usage of the facility and will go by rule of thumb and charge what the market will bear. It is only when the club has to hire a facility for its players' use that it realises the actual cost of carrying out an activity. Direct costs to be met include:

— official fees, e.g. referees, umpires;
— use of equipment, e.g. balls;
— refreshments if provided;
— playing surface costs, e.g. court fees, pitch costs;
— travelling costs of players.

Clubs should also be able to calculate the indirect cost associated with the activities being carried out. These include the cost of heating, rent, rates, loan interest. If these were apportioned directly to match fees (or subscriptions), players would have to pay out considerably more than they currently do. As an example—with local authority provision of swimming, the subsidy is well over £1 per swim what the swimmer has to pay.

If the club is able to calculate the true cost per player per match, it would be a salutary indication of how important other fund raising, such as the bar profits, is in keeping down costs to players. It would also be useful information to use when approaching outside bodies to request financial assistance for the club. Some local authorities do not give rate relief to clubs who have licensed bars for example.

It is important that players are informed of the level of match fees and if increases are necessary during a season they should be given prior notice and if possible the reasons for the increase. One problem which has arisen in recent years has been the increase in cost of travelling to matches, mainly brought about by higher petrol costs and public transport fares. It would be a good idea if match fees could be structured to allow those members who provide transport for other members of the team to be given some form of assistance. A mileage allowance towards petrol costs could be a possible solution.

Unless there are good reasons, match fees should only be levied for home matches, i.e. on those players using the club's facilities and not when the player uses other club's facilities. A record of fees collected should be kept by an appropriate person and monies handed to the treasurer for banking at the earliest possible moment.

Assistance from local authorities
It is important for sports clubs to realise that assistance which is given by local authorities varies throughout the country. Although there is certain mandatory assistance which is available e.g., to charitable recreation clubs and which may be augmented by the local authority, there are also discretionary powers which may or may not be exercised.

It is important for clubs to build up a good relationship, wherever possible with not only the political representatives on the different tiers of local government but also with their paid advisors: the officers of the local authority. Contacts should also be built up with the appropriate Member(s) of Parliament.

A study which was carried out into financial assistance available to sport clubs from local authorities identified the following tiers of government which could offer assistance:

— parish/town council;
— district council;
— county council;
— metropolitan authority;
— new town and development corporations.

Aid can be given in four ways:

— grant;
— loans;
— rate relief;

2. FINANCIAL ASPECTS OF A CLUB

— aid in kind, e.g. concessions or free use of facilities or council staff time.

The legislation under which this assistance can be offered is:

Grants
- the Physical Training and Recreation Act 1937;
- Section 137 of the Local Government Act 1972 which can give the product of up to 2p in the £ rate;
- Section 14, the 1970 GLC General Powers Act in the GLC area.

Loans
- Sections 1(i) and 2, Physical Training and Recreation Act 1958;
- local authorities can often guarantee loans offered to clubs by third parties, e.g. a bank or brewery or the Sports Council.

Rate relief. The General Rate Act 1967 (Section 40(1)) allows 50 per cent mandatory rate relief to educational premises and charities. Under Section 40(5) of the same legislation discretionary relief can be offered to sports clubs.

Some clubs only receive assistance if they have no licensed bar. If assistance for this reason is substantial, it may be cost effective for a club to arrange for post match hospitality to be offered in a local public house, hotel or other licensed premises. There are some advantages in not having a bar: e.g. a premises does not appear so tempting to professional burglars if there is no alcohol or cigarettes on the premises; no bar staff or club members have to run a bar.

If a club requires an occasional bar licence for a function, a friendly publican may apply for it; in return he would supply the alcoholic drink. Alternatively, a club may apply itself (up to four times a year) to the licensing justices for an occasional permission to sell alcohol at a function.

Assistance in kind. This is often carried out on an ad-hoc basis and can include the loan of equipment or labour to cut grass pitches or free use of changing rooms.

Criteria used to justify assistance to clubs. Clubs should try to identify the criteria which is used by local authorities when they assist clubs. Here is a list of possible criteria:

- provision of facilities for local residents;
- assistance for youth groups;
- assistance for capital projects;
- assistance towards running costs;
- assistance for certain sports;
- assistance for small clubs;
- assistance for clubs without licensed bars;

53

— assistance for indoor or outdoor facilities;
— assistance only for clubs not being helped by other bodies.

A club should try to see if other clubs in the same authority are being assisted, also they should see what the policy of neighbouring authorities is towards clubs of the same nature.

Club lobbying. It has to be accepted that if an authority is not willing to assist the easiest action is to give up. My advice is *do not.* Pressure should be brought by every means possible—get the councillors and/ or the officers interested in the club and its functions. Campaign in the local newspapers, lobby councillors—try to make informal deals, invite them to social events. Involve the Members of Parliament. In the end the hard work may pay off, and if it results in a 50 per cent rate relief being granted, or the loan of a tractor and mowing vehicle by the council it will have been worthwhile.

Prize money
With the growth in sponsored events the possibility of earning a large income from prize money is increasing. In most sports there is at least one competition which offers financial rewards for doing well.

Success tends to go in cycles and clubs would be advised not to forecast regular income from winning competitions. This source of income should be seen as an added bonus and the money received is best used for a specific project with which all members can identify— assistance towards a new facility, the reduction of a bank loan.

Sale of goods
The range of goods which can be sold by a sports club can be wide and include:

— alcoholic drinks;
— non-alcoholic drinks;
— tobacco;
— food;
— sports equipment;
— clothing and bags;
— books and magazines;
— first aid equipment;
— club and governing body insignia.

The first four items have already been dealt with in this chapter. So how can a club best supply its members with the remaining types of good?

The main decision is whether to have the goods in separate locations or at one selling point. For reasons of stock control, security and savings on staff resources one site should be designated for selling goods.

2. FINANCIAL ASPECTS OF A CLUB

The club's other decision is whether the club itself should sell the goods or bring in an outsider, e.g. a local sport shop, or whether a mix of the two should be implemented.

The turnover will be very important as it is unlikely that a small club will be attractive enough for a sports shop to stock and sell in the club. On the other hand, a club with a potential high sales projection will attract a shop to be set up at the club, e.g. the professional shop at a golf club. If a club makes its facilities available to a commercial operator it should negotiate to take a percentage of sales, e.g. 10 per cent of turnover.

Perhaps the best solution for most clubs is only to sell club and governing body material themselves, e.g. club blazers, ties and manuals, and small items of equipment, e.g. balls, with the club taking the entire profit. Other items such as sports equipment, books and magazines could be sold off the site at a discount to club members. Once again the club will avoid tying up its capital in goods which may be slow sellers.

It is unlikely that much profit will be made on club goods until a large number of items have been sold, as the cost of preparing shirts and blazers etc. with individual club insignia is very high at the outset. It may be advisable to gauge members' interest in this type of good before it is introduced. The question of fashion should also be taken into account. One club had 500 ties produced; unfortunately they were of the old "kipper" variety and when narrow ties became fashionable they were not popular and very few were sold with a large loss for the club.

Hire of club facilities

Many clubs add to their income by allowing their facilities to be used by individuals, groups, clubs and societies whose members are not members of the club.

If the club's facilities are being used by outsiders, there are several points to remember:

— the club should deal with only one person from the user organisation to ensure good communication;
— insurance implications should be examined and premiums, if necessary, be increased;
— wherever possible there should be no conflict in the use of club facilities between members and outsiders; members' needs should be paramount;
— club rules should allow outside use of facilities;
— the bar licensing position should be clear when outsiders use the club;
— one officer of the club should be responsible for contacting possible user organisations.

2. FINANCIAL ASPECTS OF A CLUB

User groups. The following users may be interested in a club's facilities:

- youth organisations, e.g. Girl Guides, Boy Scouts, who will probably want to use a hall and/or pitches in the early evening and at the weekend (the bar must be made "out of bounds");
- hobbies groups, e.g. vintage motorcycle club, chess club, who would use indoor facilities mainly including the bar and a kitchen;
- mother and toddler groups for which an adequate storage room should be available. Insurance and cleaning may be the biggest problems;

(Courtesy the Sports Council)

Sports facilities can be used for other activities by the installation of other portable equipment and protective floor covering. The illustration shows a hall being used for a children's play-group. Note the amount of adult supervision required.

- senior citizens' groups for which adequate heating and tables and chairs may be the main requirements. Medical equipment should be easily available;
- charitable groups, e.g. Rotary Club, Masonic Lodges. Meetings and talks will be followed by refreshments. Privacy will be paramount and club members should intrude as little as possible;
- educational institutions, e.g. schools, universities which could be encouraged to use playing facilities and changing rooms at off peak. Vandalism is the biggest problem;
- local industry and commerce. As well as providing resources for employees, firms may wish to hold conferences or launch new products at a club;

— tenants' and residents' associations who could hold periodic meetings followed by a social evening;

— other sports clubs and also governing bodies of sport for representative games and coaching courses;

— local authorities. Club facilities could augment those offered by a local authority when they organise an event—a chance to impress politicians, national agencies such as the Sports Council, Countryside Commission. By offering to stage events a club would be seen in a good light.

Charges could vary between the different user groups. Senior citizens' groups may not be able to afford as much as commercial or industrial concerns. Political groups should not be allowed to use club facilities for political meetings as this may (unfairly) identify the club with a certain view which may not be acceptable to some members or to the local community.

Use of facilities. Some of the users of club facilities have been identified above. But there are of course many other uses to which facilities could be put:

— the club's car park used by commercial firms during the week;

— the playing facilities used off-peak by schools and firms;

— the hall used for parties, meetings, jumble sales, pre-school playgroups, aerobics classes;

— the bar and/or catering facilities for social functions;

— the changing accommodation for tournaments organised at other locations by the local authority or other clubs.

Implications of hiring facilities. The main benefit to a club of hiring out a facility is that it generates additional income, especially if the facility is being under used or not used at all at an identifiable time, e.g. squash courts in the morning or mid-afternoon. If the facility is being used responsibly by outsiders, the club is being occupied and the risk of theft or damage by vandalism is reduced. The club may attract membership from those outsiders who use it.

There are three main *disadvantages* of allowing outsiders the use of a club's facilities:

— no direct control over individual users—the club is reliant on the organiser of the user group;

— the club's facilities may be excessively worn, for instance the use of grass pitches must be closely monitored;

— club members may not be able to use a facility if it is used by outsiders. To minimise possible friction, members should be advised in advance when facilities will not be available.

Advertising the club's facilities. If a club decides it wants its facilities to be used by outsiders, the following methods of attracting them could be used:

— sending letters listing facilities to local firms, schools, local authorities, other clubs, sport bodies, resource centres;
— advertising on the local radio and in the local newspaper either directly or by "feeding" them news items, sending the local library brochures;
— holding functions or open days to which the public is invited to attend;
— encouraging members to "spread the gospel" at their place of work or amongst their friends and contacts;
— talking to local groups such as the rotary club with visual aids such as slides or videos.

Responsibility for organising publicity of the club's facilities should rest with the publicity and public relations committee with different members taking on certain jobs. There will have to be liaison with other committees. Whatever method is adopted the information given about the club should be accurate, clearly and easily understood and attractively packaged. Standard hire prices should not be given; by not doing this the club will be free to vary its charges if it wishes. If a club member is involved in advertising, public speaking or selling he may be best suited for promoting the club's interests.

Donations, sponsorship and advertising

Donations. Normally the revenue from donations towards running costs will be very low. Donations are more willingly given if capital or large scale projects are being undertaken. Members or outside organisations would normally prefer that any donation is towards something specific, such as a new pavilion, rather than for paying bills. There is more prestige to be gathered, and possibly a plaque acknowledging aid on a wall of a new building is attractive. Some members or local authorities may, however, like to make a contribution especially if there is a deficit between yearly income and expenditure. Examples of a Vice-President writing a cheque at an Annual General Meeting to meet a club's losses are still known.

Sponsorship. Increasingly, sport is being identified by industry and commerce as an attractive vehicle through which they may project their image. Not only can its "clean" image help to increase sales and improve profits, but it is a way through which they can gain prestige and be seen as making a contribution to the good of society.

As well as large national events, e.g. the Prudential cricket test as bar takings and subscriptions. It is also advisable to have a deposit account with either a bank or building society in which money can be "stored" to meet unexpected expenditure, such as an emergency repair bill or the purchase of a new tractor. The deposit account can also be used to pay for large planned items of expenditure—new judo mats, resurfaced tennis courts etc. The rates vary between financial institutions as do the conditions of withdrawal. A higher rate of interest will normally incur a longer notice of withdrawal.

Clubs should be flexible in their approach and regularly compare rates of interest which are included in the financial pages of the Saturday morning national newspapers. If in doubt a club should consult an accountant for expert advice. If easy access of money and high interest rate can be combined in a responsible institution this is the ideal.

Clubs may also own stocks and shares. They should remember that commission will be charged on transactions. The club's bank is a good source of information about this type of investment.

Social events

As we saw in Chapter One, sports clubs are important for their social as well as for their playing activities. In fact very often it is the revenue received from social functions which enables the playing activities to either take place at all, or at a reasonable cost to the participants.

Principles of regular social events. Social events should be aimed at either breaking even or making a profit. If they are loss making there should be a very good reason for staging the event. They should be well-publicised and well-organised to be popular and attractive to members. Some events will lend themselves to regular programming and include the firework party, Christmas party, midsummer ball. The organisers—usually the social committee or its equivalent—should remember to give suppliers as much notice as possible; fireworks displays for instance have to be ordered at least nine months in advance. Tickets should be available for sale to members as early as possible to allow the maximum number to be approached.

Examples of social events. The following are examples of social events which could raise funds:

Jumble sale. It is better if this is held in the clubhouse so that additional profit can be made from selling refreshments. Charge an entrance fee and have the residue removed by a dealer.

Garden fete or party. A summer event to be opened by a celebrity. Remember pluvial insurance and check public liability insurance cover.

61

"Now they're thinking of 'sponsored throws' for a new juke box!"

Video racenight. An evening where revenue can be made on the bar and on food and from a raffle.

Disco, squaredance, ballroom dancing. Book live music or disco early. A music "theme" event is increasingly popular, e.g. '60s disco.

Fashion show. Possibly with sport as a theme—this could be popular with men and women. A commission for the club on sales.

Fancy dress party. E.g. "punk", pyjama or tarts and vicars. If a video is taken of the party it could form the basis of a social event shortly afterwards.

Pumpkin fair. To be held near halloween (31st October); prizes for the best mask.

Auction. A once a year event for bigger clubs. The level of revenue will vary with the quality of items.

Annual dinner. This should preferably be held in the clubhouse unless numbers are likely to be too great. Additional revenue on the bar and raffle.

Car rally. Care should be taken that restrictions are not broken. Speed is not of the essence;

Car boot sale. A growing phenomenon. Booking fee should be less if paid in advance. Check that no by-law is breached by Sunday trading.

Hair cutting session. This should be done either by a local salon or by members' wives.

Sponsored bounce (gymnastics clubs). Good profit is possible because of the low outlay.

Carol singing evening. This can be conducted at the club or by groups going around the vicinity. A low expenditure event with modest returns.

Barbecue. A summer activity. Normally there is a heavy outlay, e.g. tickets, food, band or disco, but with good ticket sales profit can be high.

Caribbean evening. With a steel band.

Pram race. This may appeal to younger members. If it takes place on the roads the police must be informed; better if it is contested at the club.

Whist drive. A traditional event which will appeal more to older members. Little profit will be made.

Sherry party (bubbly and strawberry evening). As drink can normally be supplied on a sale or return basis and special food-stuffs can be purchased in bulk, high profits are possible.

Puppet show. As this is aimed at children ticket prices should be low with little profit expected.

Pie and mash night. Quite a good moneyspinner. A microwave cooker will ensure that waste is kept to a minimum.

Cabaret evening. Clubs would be advised to start with a modest promotion to iron out any problems and check that the demand warrants a larger act.

Firework party and display. A large outlay but good profits are possible if tickets sell well. Safety precautions are paramount.

Fun Olympic day. The outlay is quite high with much organisation needed, large numbers of spectators can be expected especially if other clubs compete.

Donkey derby. A big crowd puller.

Crafts fair. Well presented it can be a big profit earner.

Sale of members' goods with commission to the club.

Level of profit. Costs will be reduced if the club uses its own facilities and does not hire facilities for the event. Every ancillary avenue of raising cash should be explored. The main sources are:

— the bar;
— catering;
— raffles (for regulations see Chapter Five).

Some events such as a firework party or a fun olympic day will require a large expenditure in advance ("up front money") and if a club has limited resources it may wish to concentrate on events, e.g. jumble sales which require no or little prepayment.

It is impossible to give costs for every type of event as these vary with the nature of the event and locality of the club. The following are guidelines:

— hire of disco with disc-jockey £50–£75;
— cost of large firework display £500–£750;
— cost of hiring a live band £150–£300.

Some of the events can raise a large amount of money, for instance a jumble sale or dance could show a profit of several hundred pounds; others such as the car rally will show a more modest profit. Basically, the rewards will be commensurate with the enthusiasm and efficiency of the event organisers. They should be given as much positive help as possible, for instance, a local off-licence or publican could obtain an off-licence (for details see Chapter Five) if an organisation does not have its own licensed bar.

Sometimes suppliers, such as breweries, have a marketing/promotions department which will be able to assist a club in organising an event. They can help by printing notices and tickets, donating prizes, supplying loudspeaker equipment. They will be happy to assist wherever possible as a public relations exercise, to make new contacts and help generate sales of their product.

Clubs may also like to approach other local organisations such as the church, schools, public house or newspaper to see if they are able to help the club, e.g. by lending equipment.

EXPENDITURE

Having dealt with the different categories of income which a club can obtain, the types of expenditure which a club incurs will now be examined. These can be categorised as follows:

— rent and rates;
— fuel costs;
— water and drainage;
— taxes;
— hire of facilities;
— wages and national insurance;
— repairs and general maintenance;
— insurance;
— interest payable and bank charges;
— professional fees;
— administrative costs;
— affiliation fees, officials' fees and disciplinary costs;
— publicity costs;
— cleaning and laundry;
— licences;
— transport.

2. FINANCIAL ASPECTS OF A CLUB

Rent and rates

If a club does not possess the freehold of its facilities it will either have to lease or rent them from another party, usually known as the grantor or lessor. If the property is leasehold, the club is the lessee (for other useful definitions consult Appendix B).

The level of rent for any sporting facility can vary greatly and the difference is influenced by the following factors:

— whether the lessor is private, local or public authority, or a commercial organisation (they all use different criteria when calculating rents);
— the market rate for a facility;
— the type of organisation using a facility;
— the alternative uses for the facility.

Some lessors will try to maximise their rental income, others will offer a peppercorn (nominal) rent as they wish to develop a good social image. Whenever a lease or agreement is negotiated, the rental terms will be stated. The rent review periods will usually be stated, e.g. every five years of the rental period.

It is up to the club and its representatives to negotiate the financial (and other) terms as hard as possible when the lease is being drawn up. Once it has been executed it is improbable that the terms will be varied.

Rates are levied on most property in the country and sports clubs are no exception. As we have seen, if the club is a registered charity it is entitled to at least 50 per cent mandatory rate relief from the local rating authority.

The rateable value is determined by the District Valuer who is employed by the Inland Revenue and who is independent of the rating authority. Using the figure he sets, the local authority is able to assess the rates due by multiplying the rateable value by the rate in the £ which is levied in the area as a whole. The District Valuer will inform the club and the local authority of the proposed rateable value on a hereditament (property) or extension to an existing property. It is at this stage that the club should object if it feels that the rateable value is too high. It is up to the District Valuer to argue his case at an independent tribunal. Appeals have been successful so if the club feels it has a case, it should appeal.

A club can appeal at any time if it feels its rateable value is too high. It should also request from the local rating authority a reduction if any neighbouring development adversely affects its facilities or activities.

Energy costs

The cost of energy is an increasing element in a club's budget. The clubhouse has to be heated and lit, with hot water available for washing and cooking. A club has to choose from coal, gas—natural or bottled—and electricity as its fuel source, or it can have a mixture of fuels. Often the geographical location of the club will reduce the choice. Advice on planning costs and installation will be given by the fuel suppliers who can be found in the telephone directory.

One important consideration is the usage of the club's facilities. If the club is seasonal, i.e. summer use only for cricket, it may be more appropriate for a portable heater to be used to deal with occasional use. If a full heating system is installed not only would this be costly but it would be idle in the winter—copper pipes are valuable items.

Clubs should encourage their members to be careful in their use of lights and heating and these should be switched off as much as possible to save money. Automatic cut out switches and timeswitches can be installed in areas such as the showers. Thermostatic control valves can be used on radiators and while initially they are more expensive they should save money in time.

From a study of sports clubs by the author, a club should budget for about 5 to 10 per cent of total expenditure for heating.

Water and drainage

Water and drainage are essential items which are often overlooked by clubs when drawing up their plans. Water is necessary for washing, cooking and the bar areas and is often essential for the good preparation and maintenance of outside playing areas, e.g. grass pitches and shale tennis courts.

The water companies and boards will usually install meters for payment purposes. The club should use this device as a tool for good management. If there are any unusual variations these should be investigated carefully. Once again members should be encouraged to save water by turning off taps and showers. The expected use of water should be calculated with the assistance of the appropriate water board.

Whenever possible mains drainage should be utilised; cess pits, unless they are unavoidable, have the disadvantage of having to be emptied with certain inconveniences and while being soundly constructed could cause problems if they have to be removed.

Drainage of playing facilities will be covered in Chapter Four.

Taxes

Value added tax. The main tax to which sports clubs, especially those with a licensed bar, are liable is Value Added Tax (VAT). VAT at present is charged at 15 per cent on sales and any club with a turnover in excess of £19,500 per annum must register with the local VAT office (which is part of the Customs and Excise). This level will change from time to time and the VAT office will advise accordingly.

2. FINANCIAL ASPECTS OF A CLUB

It is important for clubs to develop a good relationship with the local VAT office as it can advise the club on whether services and goods the club deals with may be exempt, zero-rated or standard rated. It will normally be the club treasurer or secretary who deals with VAT returns and it is imperative that all receipts and invoices which contain a VAT element are passed to him for safe keeping.

The VAT office issues a number of leaflets which explain the position concerning VAT, e.g. VAT leaflet No. 701/34/84 which deals with competition in sport and physical recreation, especially the question of VAT and competition entry fees.

How is VAT calculated? To charge VAT, simply add 15 per cent to the cost of a product, e.g. a club sweater with a basic price of £6 will cost £6.90 to include VAT. To calculate the VAT element of an item the club purchases simply

> multiply the price by 3/23
> to give the VAT element.

For example:
> a barrel of beer costs a club £80.
> The VAT element will be £80 × 3/23 = £10.43 VAT
> Therefore cost of goods exclusive of VAT = £80 −£10.43
> $$= £69.57$$

VAT is not chargeable on rent; a gaming machine is not subject to VAT as it is being rented by a club.

Income tax. If the club is a private members' club (it is unincorporated), the club will not have to pay income tax on any "profit" resulting from transactions between the club and members, and guests (mutual trading). It may be liable for tax if it tackles or deals with non-members, e.g. the sale of goods to visitors. A club with charitable status pays no income tax on its charitable activities.

Corporation tax. A private members' club is not liable for corporation tax on the same grounds as described above with income tax. If a club receives interest on bank deposits or building society investments, this is liable for corporation tax. As the rate of corporation tax is 30 per cent and the building society deducts 30 per cent tax at source, it is administratively easier for a club to invest its money in a building society.

Capital gains tax and capital transfer tax. Clubs are liable to all these taxes. As this is a very complex subject, clubs would be advised to contact an accountant or other adviser who is experienced in these matters. The club's bank may be able to assist but it is probable that a charge will be levied.

2. FINANCIAL ASPECTS OF A CLUB

General advice regarding taxes. The status of a club, whether it is a charity, limited company, unincorporated members' club etc. will influence the liability to pay taxes. It is advisable for clubs to discuss their situation with a local tax officer. He will be pleased to advise on the situation and he can be contacted via the telephone directory listed under Inland Revenue—Collector of Taxes.

Hire of facilities and equipment
The cost to clubs of hiring facilities, including equipment, varies with the type and size of club and the facility being used by members.

The size of a club will often influence whether outside facilities are used. A small club with a low membership is less likely to be able to sustain the cost of its own facilities and may hire facilities owned by other people. Sports which use high cost facilities, both on the capital and running side, also lend themselves to being provided with facilities for hire by an outside body. These sports include track cycling, swimming, ice skating and skiing.

The major provider of this type of facility is the local authority; normally the facilities are sited in sports centres, although the commercial sector is increasingly becoming involved in this area of business. Clubs should negotiate long term useage of hired facilities and choose off-peak periods, if possible, which will be welcomed by the owner of the facility and lower the cost to the club.

Wages and national insurance

Wages. Wages and national insurance contributions can be a large item of expenditure in a club's budget when staff are employed to carry out duties. If club members carry out duties on a voluntary basis this expenditure can be avoided or greatly reduced. Staff can be employed on either a full or part-time (casual) basis.

They can be employed as:

— groundsmen/maintenance men;
— bar staff;
— catering staff;
— security staff;
— dressing room attendant;
— paid officers such as treasurer, secretary, captain;
— club professional.

Legislation concerning the employment of staff and its implications will be dealt with in Chapter Five.

Staff selection process. Once a club has decided what staff will be needed, a budget will have to be worked out and unless outstanding candidates present themselves this should be adhered to.

2. FINANCIAL ASPECTS OF A CLUB

The following steps should be followed:

1. A job description should be formulated.
2. An employee specification should be formulated.
3. The job should be advertised.
4. An application form should be sent to candidates, though this could be omitted if there are few applicants.
5. Selected applicants should be interviewed.
6. References should be taken up about the successful candidate.
7. The successful candidate is appointed (possibly after a medical check).
8. A probation period could be worked.

As this is a complex subject and the appointment of the wrong candidate could be disastrous, club officials would be advised to appoint someone on the interviewing panel who has experience in this field. There are many books written on this subject and these are listed in the reading list (Appendix F).

As well as having an attractive salary, either in money terms alone or money terms and benefits such as accommodation, free meals, clothing etc., wages are influenced by the Wages Councils which fix minimum wages and other conditions of employment. Obviously clubs will negotiate terms with their employees but the following figures could be used for guidance:

Head groundsman = £7,216 pa (excluding accommodation)
  Source: Institute of Groundsmanship

Bar steward (works min. 34 hours per week) = £68.63 per week category 2 (with accommodation, outside London)
  Source: Office of Wages Council

Details of the wages laid down by the relevant Wages Councils' orders affecting clubs are obtainable from the Office of Wages Councils.

If a club is offering an employee a franchise for any service, e.g. catering to be sold, it would be advisable for this to be on a trial period of say six months and then to be renewed for fixed periods, e.g. yearly, three yearly etc. The club should specify what is to be offered as the service with one officer dealing with the franchisee. Accounts should be easily available and perhaps if a certain profit is exceeded the club may be entitled to a percentage of this excess.

PAYE and national insurances. Because of the complexity of this subject, it would be advisable for the appropriate club official to discuss these topics with the local Inland Revenue office and Department of Health and Social Security who will provide a number of explanatory leaflets including:

Employer's Guide to National Insurance Contributions (NP15)
Employer's Guide to PAYE (P7)
National Insurance Contribution Rates (NI208)
National Insurance Guide for Employers (NI40)

These leaflets should be available at the local library or from the offices of the DHSS.

It should be appreciated that this is a time consuming activity, especially at year end, i.e. after 5 April of each year.

Repairs and general maintenance

It is important for clubs to realise, and they possibly do already, that facilities will need maintenance to keep them functioning correctly. This expenditure will vary from club to club, depending on the facilities which the club possess. One advantage of hiring facilities is that bills for repairs and maintenance will be less than those incurred by a comparable club which owns its own facilities.

Allowance for this budgeting is essential and it is interesting to note that the Sports Council, when considering applications from clubs for grants or loans will not normally approve repairs and general maintenance items for assistance, the argument being that the club should have foreseen expenditure on this type of item as being normal in the run of events. Items which will wear out quickest should be identified and provision for replacing these made first. The variation in time period needed to provide for these items can be seen from the accounting practice of discounting or depreciating certain items over different periods.

Clubs should, if they are employing outside contractors to carry out repairs and maintenance work, try to obtain competitive tenders for the work. If the work can be carried out satisfactorily at a price which gives value for money by a club member, the contract should be given to him or her. Loyalty to members by the club is as important as loyalty by members to the club.

Insurance

"Get the strength of the insurance company around you." Although only an advertising slogan, it is a concept which should be adopted by any prudent club.

As well as insuring the club's premises, stock, ancillary machines and equipment against all risks, it is advisable that a club be insured against personal liability which will cover claims by members of the public for damage in respect of accident on the club premises. Employers' liability is obligatory and ensures that club employees are insured for injury at work through the negligence of any other club employee or of the club (or member thereof).

2. FINANCIAL ASPECTS OF A CLUB

There are several ways in which a club can obtain information about insurance. The easiest is to approach insurance brokers who should be members of the British Insurance Brokers' Association. Whilst these brokers should be impartial offering impartial information to the club/client, it should be recognised that they wish to maximise their income. Therefore they will try to sell as much insurance as possible and commission will vary from company to company. It will be best to approach several brokers for quotations. Brokers do have a major advantage in that they are experienced at handling claims and in some cases will be able to guide a club to maximise the value of the claim.

Alternatively, if a club member is connected with the insurance industry it may be beneficial to approach him for advice. If he is able to provide a quotation for the insurance in question this could be compared to that provided by a broker(s). The third option is to approach insurance companies direct. The disadvantage with this is that they will be remote from the club and much time may be used up in contacting the correct person who can deal best with the club's queries and needs.

The club should also draw the attention of its members to insurance which will cover them against loss whilst playing or loss of sports equipment. An example of this is the MILAS Sportsplan Insurance Policy which is linked to the LAMPS National Physiotherapy Service. For further details contact the address in Appendix C.

Interest payable and bank charges
In most instances where a club receives a loan to help finance its running costs or a new capital project it should make provision for the interest which will be charged as well as repayment of the capital cost.

Bank and brewery loans or building society mortgages will normally be secured on the club's property. These bodies do, however, consider accepting personal guarantees or a guarantee offered by a responsible body such as a local authority. Brewery loans usually carry the lowest rate of interest. The brewery loan is normally repaid on barrellage, i.e. the amount of beer, spirits or mixers which are purchased.

A loan made by the Sports Council is interest free. It is secured either by personal guarantors offered by the club or local authority guarantee and has to be repaid over five years at six monthly periods.

Some governing bodies of sport offer clubs loans; these include the Football Association, Lawn Tennis Association and Rugby Football Union. They charge different rates of interest and details of their schemes can be obtained through their county or regional office.

The National Playing Fields Association and its county affiliates offer loans for recreational facilities, mainly for children's play areas. Applications are made through the county offices whose address with relevant information can be obtained from the national headquarters (see Appendix E).

Local authorities may be able to offer loans to clubs but their interest rates will again vary. Details of their schemes will be obtainable from either the Treasurer's Department or through the Leisure/ Amenity Department.

Bank charges. Sports clubs, like other bank customers, are liable to bank charges for services rendered in respect of the account they operate. Clubs should compare charges. They will be in a better position to change banks if they have no liability to their existing bank, i.e. an outstanding loan.

Professional fees
A club would be advised to have expert advice available on all matters of a professional nature on a regular basis. These include:

— accountant/auditor;
— solicitor;
— doctor or physiotherapist (especially one with experience of sports injuries).

Other experts can be used on an ad hoc basis:

— groundsman;
— sports management consultant;
— architect;
— structural engineer.

The relevant institute will be able to advise on a scale of fees, e.g. for the annual auditing of the club books, improvement to the club ground etc. If expertise can be found within the club, obviously the cost will be reduced or eliminated.

Administrative costs
Often administrative costs in a club's accounts are covered by a global figure and this can be unsatisfactory. Often members are unclear what administrative costs have been incurred and consequently financial monitoring may not be carried out accurately.

The following costs will be incurred:

— postage;
— telephone calls;
— hospitality and officials' expenses, e.g. petrol;
— secretarial services.

2. FINANCIAL ASPECTS OF A CLUB

Clubs should try to reduce these costs; here are some ways in which this could be achieved:

1. Send out letters, circulars etc. second class instead of first class. If possible, correspondence could be delivered by hand using volunteers.
2. Telephone calls should be made at cheap or off-peak periods and they should be kept as short as possible.
3. All hospitality events should be examined and expenses claimed scrutinised carefully to see if value for money is being achieved.
4. Secretarial services could be modernised by using electric type-writers, computers attached to word processors to prepare subscriptions and salaries records, stock data, mailing lists.

The sale of the club membership list to outside organisations could be used to raise revenue but this must be agreed by club members, either at an annual general meeting or individually, because of the possible invasion of privacy.

Affiliation fees, officials' fees, entry fees and disciplinary costs

Affiliation fees. As Chapter One discussed, it is advisable, and normally essential, for a club to affiliate to its governing body of sport. This will allow it to compete in competitions organised under the jurisdiction of the governing body. Players will be eligible for representative matches and will be accepted on courses to become officials. Also, by affiliating the club is able to draw on technical advice, literature and administrative support offered by the governing body.

All these services have to be paid for and the affiliation fee varies between sports—for instance in squash it is per court, in hockey it is per team. The affiliation fee should be included in a player's subscription and stated clearly.

Although there is no overall policy concerning an affiliation fee to a local sports council, a club may find it advisable to make a small donation to help cover administrative and running costs.

Officials' fees. If a club uses referees, umpires or coaches from outside its own membership, it is likely they will be entitled to remuneration for their services. They may also claim for travelling expenses. One way to reduce this cost is to make the official(s) welcome before, during and after a match in which he has officiated. In this way they will look forward to helping the club and are more likely to waive their fees to do so.

The cost of a coaching or demonstration course can be minimised wherever practically possible, by inviting outside people to attend the event.

2. FINANCIAL ASPECTS OF A CLUB

Often a voluntary organisation such as the Red Cross or St John Ambulance Brigade will attend matches to assist with medical problems which may arise. A club should ensure that they receive a donation either after each match or at the end of the season. The appropriate amount will depend on the cover provided; the organisation providing a caravan should be given more than that providing one officer.

Entry fees. It would be most unusual for any sports club not to want to enter competitions, either in a team context or through individual members of a club. Although many competitions, tournaments etc. receive sponsorships, most require an entry fee to help offset costs and to ensure that entrants are serious in their intent to compete. Most entry fees have to be paid at the time of application. To reduce the burden on club finances, entry fees could be paid for either partly or wholly by the individuals concerned.

Disciplinary costs. With the pressures of the modern game and the growing tendency to question decisions which are given by sports' officials, there has been a rise in the number of fines and penalties which are levied on offenders against the rules, and in extreme cases against the clubs themselves.

If fines are meted out, then it should be the offender who should pay. If the club does, all members are subsidising foul play or behaviour and the club is seen as condoning this state of affairs. However, if a club, and its relevant committee, feel that a member is being treated badly it should consider assisting a player in his case.

Publicity costs

As discussed before, some of the costs of publicising the club's facilities and activities can be reduced by sponsorship, e.g. firms' names on match cards and in membership cards/books. Other methods which can be employed are:

1. "Feed" news items to local newspapers about the club rather than paying for advertisements. Often a local newspaper will carry an advert, especially at the beginning of the season, free of charge.
2. Handbills or notices about the club can be delivered by volunteer club members rather than being posted to people living in the vicinity.
3. Hand drawn posters could be prepared rather than printed for distribution to local shops, pubs, libraries etc. rather than using professionally prepared notices. These should be neatly produced to achieve best results.
4. The community service section of local radio (independent or

BBC) could be given details of club events. A series of adverts would be expensive.

5. Instead of paying the motoring organisations (the AA and RAC) to affix road signs advertising a special event, signs could be ingeniously sited, e.g. on the roof rack of a car parked near the club's entrance, or attached to trees the night before an event showing where it is taking place. These should be removed immediately after the end of the event to minimise inconvenience and also to allow them to be used again. Flyposting is not to be recommended as it is illegal and the club could be prosecuted. Members should be advised accordingly.

Cleaning and laundry

Cleaning. A club should try to present its best "face" to its members and to non-members. Even if its facilities are not expensive or the newest, by keeping them clean and tidy its image can be enhanced. While in catering in the club context people eat mainly "with their eyes" so the general impression of the club atmosphere will encourage goodwill towards the club. Very often for instance a clean building will deter vandalism and graffiti; a scruffy building may do the opposite. To reduce costs of cleaning the building, machines such as industrial vacuum cleaners and floorpolishers may have to be purchased. Although these have a higher capital cost than the domestic version they are capable of coping with a greater workload in a shorter time.

When the clubhouse is being planned or altered, materials that allow easier cleaning should be chosen. Shower rooms should be built with non-slip tiles and metal towel and grab rails.

Cleaning the club's premises could be carried out by its members, paid employees or outside contractors. If members are not able to do this work the cost of employees against contractors should be compared. Club members can help to minimise the cost and time associated with cleanliness, e.g. muddy boots should be removed outside the clubhouse. In the bar, ashtrays and waste baskets should be used.

Laundry. Not only does a well dressed team look "professional" with a possible psychological advantage over scruffy opponents but it helps a club's image. It may also be in the rules of a competition that club colours should be worn during all matches.

The question of cleaning playing kit can be solved in three ways:

— the player has responsibility for his own kit;
— one person possibly on a rota system can be responsible for cleaning his side's strip;

— an outside laundry can be used.

Although the first option is the cheapest it does lead to difficulties if a player is dropped from a side and a replacement does not have the appropriate shirt, socks etc. Normally this problem only applies to a first or second team so a good solution would be to choose the second or third option for those sides, and let other team players launder their own kit.

In fairness, members of the first and second teams should make a contribution through their match fees to either reimburse a member or pay an outside laundry to carry out the work. In this way other club members are not subsidising them in addition to cleaning their own muddy togs.

Licences

There are a number of licences which a club should possess, failure of which may result in prosecution, with appropriate penalties. As the position will vary from club to club, it would be advisable if the appropriate issuing body is consulted at the earliest stage. Their addresses are given in Appendix E.

Security of tenure. If a licence is necessary to use a facility, e.g. a playing area, the details such as cost and length of time of validity etc. are agreed with the licensor before it becomes effective.

Music, singing, dancing. A licence is applied for at the appropriate magistrates court.

Sale of intoxicating liquor. As above.

Performance of music, whether live or recorded. A licence is granted by the Performing Rights Society (PRS). Clubs qualify under the cost tariff J, details of which are contained in the PRS yearbook. One of their local licensing inspectors will be able to advise and these are contacted through the PRS headquarters.

Use of a television. A licence for either a colour or a black and white set is obtainable from the Post Office.

Use of a motor vehicle. A road fund licence can be purchased for either a six or twelve month period. The details of licensing and taxation for minibuses or coaches can be obtained from the Department of Transport's Traffic Areas. A useful free booklet issued by the Department is a Guide to the Licensing of Public Service Vehicles and can be obtained from the Traffic Area Office.

2. FINANCIAL ASPECTS OF A CLUB

Club transport

There are three modes of transport which the club can use. These are air, water and land. Unless a club is involved in very long distances, especially abroad, it is most likely that transport methods on land will be used.

International travel. If international travel is scheduled the best progress would be made by approaching a travel agent who has experience of sport and who knows a club's needs and the problems it is likely to encounter. Sources of information are the Central Council of Physical Recreation, the governing body of sport and the Association of British Travel Agents, or through advertisements placed in newspapers or sports magazines. Clubs will need to give plenty of advance notice of the travel times, numbers involved and standard of accommodation required. If any bulky or awkwardly shaped equipment has to be transported this should also be stated. Sometimes a club can "twin" with a foreign club and savings on accommodation can be made if players stay with club members. Hospitality should be reciprocated.

Domestic travel. The most flexible form of domestic travel is by road. Although rail and air have a time advantage over long distances, there is the question of access to and from the major embarkation points and a change to a second form of vehicle is usually necessary.

Road travel. Although a club should choose between providing transport for club members on club business from its own resources or through hiring vehicles such as coaches for certain occasions, there will be many factors which should be taken into account.

Financial factors. If a club purchases a vehicle, the result will be that its capital will immediately be tied up and the usage of such vehicle may not be as envisaged. Maintenance and safekeeping of the vehicle must be arranged for legal and insurance purposes and appropriate licences and insurances purchased. In some clubs, certain members may not be able to take advantage of the vehicle and they will be in effect subsidising those that do.

Club members may arrange a car rota system for matches, normally "away" fixtures, and while this can be complicated to administer with mileage allowances it does have the advantage to the club that those using cars are subsidised by other members and the costs of vehicles, licences, insurance etc. do not fall on the club.

Non-financial factors. Some clubs may need a "communal" vehicle to enable them to take part in matches or competitions. These clubs may be located in isolated locations or have a predominance of young or very old members—these groups having a low car ownership level—or they may be badly served by public transport. The frequency of events in which transport is needed and the distances and standard of fixtures should also be taken into account. Finally, if a coach is used it does mean that players and/or supporters can enjoy themselves without falling foul of the breathalyser!

Clubs must look at the cost implications of methods of transport very closely. The best solution may be a mix of systems—for instance, a members' car rota for local matches but the hire of a coach for long distance games, such as national cup competitions. In higher competition it is important that players do not arrive tired for the match, and by using a coach driver fatigue will be eliminated.

Security precautions

Unfortunately, sports clubs are not immune from the current trends of crime and violence. Problems range from pilfering in changing rooms and graffiti daubed on walls, to more serious crimes such as armed robbery and arson.

When clubs are planning their facilities, it is advisable that they incorporate security systems at an early stage. The best person to consult is the crime prevention officer at the local police station. Some precautions spring readily to mind:

1. Burglar alarms, preferably linked direct to the police station.
2. Security shutters or grilles on the outside of the building (windows and entrances), and inside the building on sensitive areas such as the bar.
3. Lockable rooms and safes where valuables can be stored.
4. Identifying marks put on expensive equipment.
5. Security areas for machines, including telephones, which retain cash.
6. Robust lockers in changing areas and in social areas.
7. Floodlighting externally to reduce vandalism.
8. Ease of access to a telephone for those on duty in the bar in case of trouble.
9. The presence of some form of restraining influence, whether physical or moral at social events especially if non-members are present.

Many of these precautions will be required by the club's insurance company before it will offer cover against certain risks. Although these precautions will add to the club's ongoing costs, they should be implemented in order to safeguard the club's and members' property.

Summary
Financial Aspects of a Club

1. Day-to-day financial matters and short term planning
Clubs need to examine their normal financial matters to ensure that they are being effectively conducted in order to allow activities to be carried out and short term requirements planned for.

2. Club income
Revenue can be derived from many sources including:
subscriptions;
bar receipts;
sale of goods;
receipts from machines;
hire of club facilities to outsiders;
social events.

The maximisation from these sources is investigated with alternatives examined, e.g. possible categories of membership are examined, the profitability and operation of the licensed bar, the value of catering.

Sources of aid from local government are described together with the current legislation and procedure for rate relief. Different fundraising events are discussed with guidelines and advice on advertising revenue also detailed.

3. Club expenditure
Expenditure is necessary on many different items. These include:
rent and rates;
fuel;
wages and national insurance;
repairs;
insurance.

As well as suggesting ways in which these can be minimised, questions about how VAT is calculated and a process for selecting staff are also examined.

3
Funding Large Projects

"It's no go the picture palace, it's no go the stadium
It's no go the country cot, with a pot of pink geraniums
It's no go the government grant, it's no go the elections."

Before we examine in Chapter Four how clubs should go about the planning and installation of new large or capital projects, we should discuss how they can be funded and hopefully disprove the last of the lines above by Louis Macneice.

FINANCIAL CONSIDERATIONS

It cannot be repeated enough that a club should make a plan or feasibility study into the facilities it wants or needs. Financial planning will indicate precisely what is required—purchase of site, construction of a new building, improvement of pitches or provision of large items of equipment.

The type of financial questions which need consideration include:

Will the rates increase and by how much?
Will overall expenditure be altered?
Will insurance premiums be increased?
Will extra security have to be provided?
Will additional staff costs be incurred?
Will subscriptions be increased to meet the costs, or can sufficient money be generated to avoid an additional burden on members?

Some of these questions will be answered more easily than others, for example, insurance premium quotations can be more accurately quoted than the overall costs of heating, lighting and maintenance. Similarly, the cost of additional security alarms, or guards should be easier to forecast than any rate burden.

The planning of a new facility should be the responsibility of a subcommittee set up with appropriate expertise. It can obtain useful advice from many sources including:

— the contractors or suppliers;
— the regional office of the Sports Council;

3. FUNDING LARGE PROJECTS

— the local authority (for rates information);
— other clubs with similar facilities;
— public utilities which provide power and water;
— governing body of the sport.

Once the planning sub-committee has had its recommended choice of facility (and it should examine the maximum practical possibilities) endorsed by the general club membership, the process of providing the facility should be started as soon as possible. This will minimise increases in costs and utilise the new found enthusiasm of club members, who, if wheels are not set in motion, may soon lose interest in a project.

Because of the variation in size, facilities and resources of clubs, each capital project will involve a different approach. For example, a club with a large membership of 1,000 plus may not find it difficult to fund a project costing £2,000; to a small club with only 25 members this will be a colossal undertaking. Some organisations such as the Sports Council do set down criteria for capital projects and these have to cost in excess of £1,000 to qualify under their capital grants scheme. Projects with a lower cost are eligible for assistance, however, under a different grant heading.

If a club does not plan a large project correctly, a costly burden may be placed on it in the future, e.g. a glass-backed exhibition squash court which attracts no tournaments is not the best use of funds for a club.

Often a project is only feasible if financial or practical assistance from external sources is added to the club's funds. Clubs should note that most funding agencies require a certain element of self-help over projects. Agencies have more requests for assistance than they can provide help for at most times.

CLUBS' OWN EFFORTS

Normally, a fund raising sub-committee will be set up to raise finance for a project. Many of the ideas for increasing revenue which were included in Chapter Three can be adopted when considering the financing of a large project. As the revenue from these sources will be needed for normal running costs, additional methods should be considered:

— loans or donations from club members;
— sale of "bricks";
— club acting as building society agency;
— collection and sale of paper and scrap;
— 100 club;

Renewed and upgraded spectator terracing at Wakefield Sports Club. This was part of a project carried out by Community Industry sponsored by the club's own rugby section.

— sale of life memberships;
— celebrity sports event;
— ordinary sports event, e.g. sponsored walk, marathon, tournament.

Before looking at these different possibilities, the organisers should remember that for them to be successful there have to be the three key elements:

— time;
— money;
— organisation.

augmented by a fourth—information.

At the onset of the fund raising effort, all present and past club members should be informed both by poster in the club and also by written communication what has to be achieved and the goal in mind, e.g. a new clubhouse, floodlit all-weather tennis court. Perhaps some form of "barometer", as used outside churches being renovated, could be set up so that the progress of fund raising can be visible, but wait until at least 10 to 25 per cent has been raised. A social evening could also be held with the local press and possible contributors invited. Not only will publicity and interest be generated but some donations should be forthcoming and bar takings increased by the event.

News on progress about the appeal and the new facilities should be transmitted, say, when it is half finished and then during completion. As many people as possible should be involved with the scheme, the work not being left to a few willing "horses".

Club members' loans and donations

Members can be asked to subscribe money directly by making a donation to the club. Alternatively, there can be a levy on subscriptions, or both methods can be used. The levy on subscriptions is much fairer as all members will be financially involved and not just those who have some disposable income. A subscription levy, if it is spread over two or three years, will encourage a continuing interest in the scheme. Once the project is complete, this element must be removed from the subscription payment.

If donations are made these should be recorded carefully, and when the project is finalised the donors could be shown on a commemorative plaque in the clubhouse. If many small donors assist the club, their names can be included in the programme which should be produced in association with any event at the end of the effort.

Loans made by members can either be interest free or paid with interest. Whichever repayment method is selected, it is important that the terms of the loan are clearly stated in the loan agreements. A deferred loan is one where repayment does not start for a period. Provision must be made for future loan repayments and any loans should not be secured on club facilities, as this could complicate negotiations with outside organisations.

A club should try to organise its income from members as this will mean that less funding has to be raised outside which will be at higher, commercial, rates of interest.

Sale of "bricks"

People enjoy the "fun" side of a new project and a novel way of expressing this is to translate their donations into the purchase of bricks or squares of turf. These are not real items but a schematic equivalent which can be diagrammatically expressed on a plan displayed in the club.

For example, a diagram of a building can be divided into "bricks", "windows", "doors", "roof tiles" and each item can have a price—brick = £1, a window = £5, a door = £10. If someone donates £10 this equals ten bricks or two windows. The name of the donor will be written into the diagram which could also be coloured in. This will give an immediate progress report on the project and show who has contributed.

The club as a building society agency

It has been known for a sports club to become an agent for a building society. For this type of scheme to be worthwhile there should be a large membership with an estimated large sum of deposits which will earn the club commission.

"You're a week early, idiot!"

There are several disadvantages and these are:

— the amount of paperwork involved;
— security of cash handling may have to be improved;
— members will have to have confidence that their financial matters are being confidentially handled.

Collection and sale of paper and scrap
The collection of old paper and scrap (including vehicle batteries) for sale to dealers is normally only profitable if large amounts are collected. Some items will be more valuable, e.g. computer paper instead of newsprint, copper instead of brass.

Arrangements will have to be made for storage and collection when a certain volume has been collected. *Yellow Pages* will list dealers who will advise on prices. As paper is inflammable, it should be kept well away from the main club buildings. As metal is valuable, it should be stored securely. If batteries are collected, care must be taken if they contain acid in their cells.

This method of fund raising, which is slow in results, is best suited to clubs with a large number of willing collectors, e.g. those with a strong junior section.

100 club
Many clubs with a large membership organise a club with a specific number of entrants (100, 200, 400) who pay an annual subscription

which is used as prize money in regular draws. The subscription can be paid annually to the club (the best method as interest is accrued) or monthly by direct debit or standing order. The prizes can be distributed on a weekly, monthly and bi-annual basis. These could be at the following rates: £10, £100 and £500.

If the annual subscription is £50 with 100 members, income is £5,000 with prizes being £2,720 (£10 × 52 + £100 × 12 + £500 × 2 = £2,720) giving a profit for club funds of £2,280.

This scheme should only be introduced if approximately 100 members will participate, as there is an onus on the club to guarantee the prizes which are advertised to members. It is easy to calculate the numbers of participants necessary to break-even. Using this example, it will be 55 members, i.e. £2,720 in prize money divided by the £50 subscription fee.

The big prizes should be drawn during an important social event, e.g. mid-summer ball and Christmas party. Details of prize-winners should be circulated to members regularly and displayed within the clubhouse, together with an appropriate supply of application forms.

Sale of life memberships
Although the category of life membership of a club may normally be available, the provision of a new facility may enhance a club enough to encourage more life members. If more life memberships are introduced the club will have a large injection of funds; measured against this will be a reduction of membership income in future years.

In calculating the fee, clubs should analyse their membership records on membership turnover and those remaining members for longer than ten years. As a rule of thumb, life membership should be the annual fee multiplied fifteen times.

Celebrity sports event
Many celebrities and famous sportsmen and women will be pleased to appear in a fund raising event for a sports club. A fee will normally be requested. Clubs can find the details of agencies from regular publications such as *Broadcast and Television Weekly* which are available from newsagents, and annuals such as *Artistes and their Agents*. The entertainments officer of the local authority—if he arranges shows for the public with stars—may also be of help. If a celebrity lives near the club, he could be contacted direct.

An alternative to contracting individuals to appear would be to play a match against a charity sports team, such as a disc jockeys' football team or an actors' cricket side. Professional teams should also be considered, e.g. a county cricket side, and the relevant secretary should be contacted; the match could be part of a player's benefit—an appearance guarantee would be requested by the county side. Whichever form the event is to take, the star attraction should be contacted as early as possible as crowd pullers are in great demand.

Once the event and celebrities have been determined, sponsorship should be sought to cover costs. Costs will be reduced if the club's facilities are used and not hired from outside sources. A programme should be printed, if possible in colour with pictures.

Ancillary activities could include:

— a band;
— a raffle;
— secondary "fun" match;
— presentation of trophies;
— guest speaker.

Ordinary sports events
There are many different types of event which can be organised by a club to raise money. These include:

— knockout tournaments;
— marathons;
— races;
— rallies etc.

Certain events will be more appropriate to different clubs; a marathon would be ideal for an athletics club, a knockout tournament for a hockey club, a rally for a cycling club.

If an event takes place within the confines of the club's ground there will be less organisational problems than when outside facilities are used. If it is in a public place, e.g. the highway, the police will have to be fully consulted and notice taken of their advice.

Checklist 2: For a successful fund raising event

Although details will vary according to the type of event, the following points should be considered by a promoter:

1. Has the club agreed that an event be organised?
2. Will the facility be available for the proposed event? For example, will a gymnastics section forego their regular use of a hall to allow a boxing section to stage a tournament?
3. Have invitations been sent out to possible participants in good time, stating the cost of entry, venue, date?
4. Has the club agreed to meet any losses in the event of insufficient income through sponsorship, programme or food sales, entry fees being raised?
5. Has the event been adequately advertised, locally or regionally?

6. Have enough officials been appointed either from within the club or from outside sources?

7. Will there be enough changing and shower accommodation for the participants? If additional space is needed the local authority could be approached to see if it can meet any overflow.

8. A club could conversely approach the local authority to see if it can provide (at a price) facilities to help at a local authority event.

9. Has additional catering been arranged? This could include mobile units such as provided by the Milk Marketing Board.

10. Has a licence for a bar extension been obtained from the licensing authority? It is best if at least one month's notice is given.

11. Have prizes such as cups and medals been ordered and a celebrity been engaged to make the awards? (The club chairman will do as a substitute—he is cheaper!)

12. Has a voluntary medical organisation been approached, in good time, to provide cover? County branch offices are listed in the telephone directory; headquarters' numbers are in Appendix E. Reserve space for an ambulance and lay on water and telephone facilities. For large or high-risk events, budget for a doctor. Volunteers should be given free refreshments and their organisation thanked during speeches and prizegiving.

13. Have signs and notices been prepared and put up in good time?

14. Has a loudspeaker system been installed and checked?

15. Have officials' match result cards been prepared together with a results notice board?

16. Has hospitality been arranged for sponsors, organisers, dignitaries etc?

17. Has the local newspaper been advised of the event and given details of participants and any attending celebrities?

18. Have helpers been given tee-shirts as a small token of thanks for their assistance?

19. Has the club's brewery been approached to help with the organisation and to present a prize (if applicable)?

20. Is the playing programme flexible enough to allow for bad weather, e.g. has an all-weather surface been booked?

21. Is spare equipment available such as paper, pencils, chalk, knife?

22. Have post-event arrangements been made, e.g. will results be telephoned and reports put into the newspaper and on local radio?

23. Has insurance of any trophies or prizes to be awarded to visiting players or teams been arranged?

24. Will local citizen band radio groups and youth groups such as boy scouts, girl guides be able to assist the promoter? If they can they should be contacted.

25. Has suitable car parking been arranged with voluntary attendants able to supervise? Flags, hailers and rope will probably be needed.

26. Have spectators' facilities such as seating, temporary toilets and marquees been planned?

Club's self help in building work

Clubs will be able to effect great savings in their scheme by doing much of the work themselves. Often equipment can be built at a fraction of the cost of manufactured items; in fact many manufactured items have to be assembled by club members before they can be used. In building schemes if there are skilled club members who can supervise volunteers tasks such as digging trenches and laying concrete should be within their scope. Decoration of the new clubhouse should also be possible. A longer list of possible self-help building tasks will be found in Appendix A.

Obviously, some jobs such as laying artificial grass pitches and providing specialised equipment such as floodlighting has to be carried out by a contractor, preferably one who is experienced in this type of job. But it is worthwhile for a club, when it is putting a job out to tender, to identify those items which it feels it is capable of carrying out itself. A contractor can then subdivide the quote into the cost for the job without club assistance and the reduced cost with it being available.

If a club shows that it is willing to do a lot of the work itself it can benefit from a higher rate of grant from the Sports Council. If it is recommended in the voluntary club grant programme, it is eligible for up to 75 per cent of the cost of the materials used rather than the normal maximum of 50 per cent of cost.

ASSISTANCE FROM OUTSIDE SOURCES

Checklist 3: For an application for grant aid

Help is available to clubs in the form of finance or provision of labour from private and public sectors. Here are some points to be considered both before and when submitting an application:

1. The planned facility and its estimated cost should be known.
2. Informal discussions with the body to whom an application is to be made should be held. Unforeseen design faults or new sources of finance may be unearthed.
3. Different organisations have different aims and the style of application should be varied with emphasis being placed on different parts of the scheme when appropriate. The Sports Council, for example, has a strategy for the 1980s, including population target groups—the over 50s and 13–25s—and sports it wishes to encour-

age in its "Concentration of Resources" programme. The emphasis changes annually and in 1983/4 included keep fit and movement and dance. The National Playing Field Association on the other hand will want to support children's play and play equipment.

4. Decisions are normally taken by committees and it would be useful to time the application so that all the papers can be considered in full by members.

5. If possible, application forms should be "professionally" submitted with details entered in typescript and be dated with signature of the responsible club official who is the contact. (His or her telephone number should also be included in the form.)

6. Full supporting documentation, clearly presented, will always assist the club. Items should be securely inserted in a folder or cover and include building plans, estimates, copies of permissions and undertakings, a site plan, cash flow projections for the club, a history of the club and the purpose of the building. Photographs can also help a committee form an impression of the project.

7. A club must be able to fulfill the conditions of the award of a grant and loan if they are awarded. Any information requested of them should be submitted as soon as possible, but if delays are anticipated the grant awarding body should be informed either by telephone or letter.

8. Organisations receive more requests for aid than they can normally satisfy. If a club is unsuccessful it can either re-apply at a later date or perhaps only ask for a part of the scheme to be considered for aid.

9. If an award is made it should not be jeopardised in any way, e.g. if work has to be started by a certain date make sure this is done even if it means a sod of earth being turned at 11.59 pm on 31 March, i.e. the last moment before a new financial year starts. Remember by the time an award is made to a club a lot of work has been done by the aiding organisation and this factor as well as a desire to help a club will guarantee it is as sympathetic as it can be; the safeguard of public or private funds is the only rider to this view (quite rightly so).

Public sources of aid

There is a wide range of sources of public aid. Some projects will be more interesting to certain sources than others; however, a club should explore all possibilities.

Financial assistance. This is available by way of grant or loan or a mix of both. The main bodies from whom financial assistance may be available are:

1. Local government: parish town councils;
                                    district councils;
                                    county councils.

3. FUNDING LARGE PROJECTS

2. Central government: Department of the Environment;
Department of Employment.

3. Agencies: The Sports Council;
development corporations;
Community Industries Ltd;
Manpower Services Commission.

There are other publicly funded organisations which are empowered to give aid but in practice the amounts set aside for voluntary sports clubs are very small and are therefore of minor importance. These organisations include:

— European Economic Community;
— Department of Education and Science;
— Home Office;
— Department of Health and Social Security;
— English Tourist Board;
— Arts Council;
— Nature Conservancy;
— Countryside Commission;
— Development Commission;
— water authorities;
— National Council for Voluntary Organisations (charity).

Local government. There is a great variation in the level of aid and encouragement given to recreation and sports clubs by local authorities. Some councils concentrate on helping with running costs, while others concentrate on assisting capital projects.

A club should, firstly, contact the clerk of the town or parish council, the principal officer of the recreations department (or its equivalent) or a district council or the clerk of the county council to find out if:

— money will be available;
— the criteria and conditions which apply;
— the date(s) by which an application has to be submitted.

It is advisable for a club to approach all three tiers, if possible, because, depending on the type and scale of the scheme, while one council may refuse to help, the others may be supportive. For a club to be considered for support by the Sports Council, and some other bodies, it must demonstrate that it has applied to the local authority in the first instance. Some authorities are automatically advised by the local sports council of applications so it is in the club's interest to be affiliated to the local council.

Central government. Department of the Environment. The department makes grants available to voluntary organisations from two

sources. Firstly, through its Urban Conservation and Historic Buildings Division for the upkeep, repair and conversion of certain
buildings and environmental schemes. Secondly, through the Urban
Programme which is divided into:

— partnership authorities;
— programme authorities;
— other designated districts;
— traditional Urban Programme.

Applications under the Urban Programme are made through local
authorities who meet 25 per cent of the cost of a project with the
balance being funded by the department. Details of these schemes and
the areas in which they can operate can be obtained from the department's Inner Cities Directorate. It publishes a booklet *The Partner-
ships at Work* which describes a selection of the projects funded
under the Urban Programme. Grants made under this programme can
include a contribution towards coaching courses and other "current"
expenditure, i.e. not capital expenditure.

Department of Employment. The department operates a Young
Workers Scheme and Job Splitting Scheme which are mainly
designed to help alleviate unemployment. If clubs would like more
details of these schemes they can contact the department for free
leaflets about them (see Appendix E for addresses).

Agencies.
The Sports Council. Set up by Royal Charter in 1972 as an independent body (although funded annually by the Department of the Environment), the Council has four aims:

1. To promote general understanding of the social importance and
   value of sport and physical recreation.
2. To increase provision of new sports facilities and stimulate fuller
   use of existing facilities.
3. To encourage wider participation in sport and physical recreation
   as a means of enjoying leisure.
4. To raise standards of performance.

Sports Council staff serve at its London headquarters, nine regional
offices and six residential National Sports Centres. As well as providing grants and interest free loans (repayable over five years) to sports
clubs the council is also able to offer technical advice.

Clubs make applications for financial assistance through the appropriate regional office which supplies the relevant application form
and advisory leaflets describing the scheme and its conditions. Applications are considered three times a year and the regional office will
advise on the relevant closing date for applications to be submitted.

3. FUNDING LARGE PROJECTS

The Sports Council can assist with the following:

— indoor sports facilities;
— outdoor sports facilities;
— specialist facilities;
— purchase of land and sporting rights;
— major (not routine) repairs;
— purchase of sports equipment (there are some exceptions);
— special facilities for the disabled (although there are exceptions);
— provision of social accommodation to complement an existing sports facility (eligible only for a loan).

A grant or loan of up to 50 per cent of approved cost of a project (except for projects in areas of special need, see below) may be given subject to an upper limit of £15,000 for grant or £10,000 for loan or a combined limit of £15,000. Where both grant and loan are given, the combined total cannot exceed 75 per cent of the cost. The minimum loan which is given is £1,000 and clubs will have to find up to ten personal guarantors or have a guarantee from a local authority as security.

The total grant contribution from public funds (e.g. local authority, Manpower Services Commission and Sports Council) will be limited to 75 per cent of cost of the project.

The District Valuer's advice will be sought in connection with the purchase of property or property rights and the grant will be based on his valuation. (In this type of application clubs should submit a clear site plan to the Sports Council.)

Because of the demand on funds, the level of aid is not normally given at the maximum levels and each application is considered on its merit. The amount which may be offered depends on the following main factors:

— value for money which is a judgment based on the building costs and relevant factors connected with a scheme;
— an assessment of the money needed to achieve the desired development (the "threshold" level);
— the relation of the costs of the facilities to the use which will be made of them;
— the extent to which the facilities will contribute to the achievement of the Sports Council's national objectives which are set for a period of time (clubs should consult the Sports Council report *Sport in the Community: the Next Ten Years* for details);
— the extent to which the provision of facilities will be consistent with regional priorities.

Within each of its regions the Sports Council will identify priorities, including:

— facilities of regional significance, e.g. used for regional competitions or training purposes;

— existence and availability of local facilities, i.e. in the close vicinity of peoples' homes;
— the greatest needs either in terms of geographic area or sections of the community.

These aims are contained within the regional strategies which have been formulated. Clubs would be advised to consult the appropriate regional office and discuss it formally with a staff representative of the council before a formal application is made.

To receive a grant or loan the following *conditions* have to be met:

— membership and access to the club must be "open to all";
— organisation is not constituted or operated for profit of its members and no assets to be distributed at any time (even on dissolution);
— adequate security for loans must be offered;
— adequate security of tenure on the club's facilities (limit of grant will vary according to length);
— reasonable cost of project;
— financial need of club;
— financial viability of club;
— no prior commitment to project before the application is approved;
— no mortgage or charge secured on facility;
— insurance of facility required;
— right of access to facility by Sports Council staff;
— right of inspection of books relating to facility by the Sports Council;
— repayment in the event of sale or breach of conditions;
— organisation must meet 25 per cent of cost from its own resources;
— no constitutional restriction on the club raising a loan.

If a club wishes to start a project before the result of an application is known, it should ask the regional office for permission to go ahead, especially if delays will lead to an increase in cost. This permission is known as "Without Prejudice Permission". Granting of this permission does not commit the council to offering financial aid to a club.

Areas of special need. Clubs which are situated in areas of special need, normally urban areas, which are characterised by features such as bad housing, high unemployment, low socio-economic groups, and disproportionate numbers of young people are eligible for Sports Council grant aid up to 75 per cent of the cost of a project. The regional office will be able to advise if a club is eligible.

If a club is going to do the work on a project itself and only needs assistance towards materials, the maximum grant level is 75 per cent of approved cost.

There are often special grant schemes in operation through which the Sports Council encourages certain provision, whether sport based or geographically based. Examples of these have been the Football and the Community Scheme, Merseyside Initiatives and the Pound for Pound programme in Newcastle and Bristol. If a club is eligible for aid of this nature again the regional office will advise.

The Sports Council likes to encourage grass roots sports schemes, especially those which will encourage participation. If a club, for example, wants to set up a coaching scheme or run a tournament especially for one of the council's target groups such as ethnic minorities or the disabled, it should contact the Sports Council for advice. If no money is forthcoming, other useful information may be gained such as suppliers of cheap equipment and facilities for hire. It is through this regional participation grant scheme that major items of expenditure costing less than £1,000 are eligible.

Development corporations. New towns and development corporations have been able to assist clubs by making direct grants or by offering attractive forms of assistance such as generous rate relief and subsidised rent. Clubs should consider locating in these areas if it will give them financial benefit which outweighs other considerations.

Community Industries Ltd. Community Industries Ltd, which is now a registered charity but funded by the Department of Employment, is able to assist clubs, who become employing sponsors, by constructing facilities for them. The club provides the materials and Community Industries provides the labour and supervises staff. There are 57 area offices, but not all the country is covered by these offices. Details of the scheme which only assists charities and voluntary organisations can be obtained from the headquarters of Community Industries. One of the results of a Community Industries scheme can be seen on page 82. The main aim of the scheme is to help disadvantaged 18 year-olds to gain work experience to assist their future prospects through temporary employment which is of benefit to the community.

Manpower Services Commission. The Manpower Services Commission administers several schemes which can be of assistance to clubs. The chief of these is the Community Programme which is designed to help long-term unemployed adults by undertaking projects which are of "benefit to the community".

If a club has a project it feels the Community Programme would be interested in, it should first have informal discussions with the local Community Programme Manager. He has to satisfy himself on points such as whether the club has adequate security of tenure, rules are not prohibitive, and as a sponsor will it be able to take on the duties of an employer, such as ensuring that the provisions of the Health and Safety at Work Act are observed. The scheme will have to be approved by an Area Manpower Board and it is important for clubs to ensure that there will be no trade union or employers' organisation objections to the project. It may be beneficial to the club if it uses a national agent or the local authority as sponsor for the project. Clubs will be advised about this by the Community Project Manager. Details of the Community Project and local addresses are contained in a free leaflet obtained from the Manpower Services Commission.

The Manpower Services Commission also runs a Voluntary Project Programme; this is very much smaller in scope and details are available from the Manpower Services Commission again in leaflet form.

Clubs should realise that if they are awarded assistance by the Manpower Services Commission under any of these schemes in return for a good job being done at small cost to the club, the time scale of the work is likely to be longer than if a firm of professionals is employed. It takes time for unemployed people to learn building skills; if delays happen the club should remember that it chose this option.

Minor government funding. The following central government departments and agencies have facilities to make grant aid available to voluntary organisations, but sports clubs projects are not normally directly assisted. Clubs benefit indirectly, e.g. by hiring halls in schools or by using improved countryside access and facilities, such as provided by the Countryside Commission or Nature Conservancy Council.

European Economic Community. Although there is a social fund administered by the EEC which gives grants which are aimed at reducing unemployment, it is very unlikely that voluntary clubs will be successful with an application. Detailsof the scheme can, however, be obtained from the Department of Employment, Overseas Division (OB2).

Department of Education and Science. Most grants made to voluntary organisations are directed towards organisations mainly for young people and also for educational purposes, e.g. field study centres.

Home Office. There is a special section of the Home Office—the Voluntary Services Unit—which exceptionally deals with aid applications where there is no relevant departmental source of funding, or where a project is within the ambit of more than one department. Because of the avenues open to clubs—the Sports Council, Urban Aid, Community Programme—it is likely that a project will fall within their responsibility and so the Voluntary Services Unit will not be able to assist. Their address is given in Appendix E.

Department of Health and Social Security. It is unlikely that sports clubs will receive much of the funding for voluntary organisations which is made by the department as the eligibility condition is that organisations should be engaged in the field of health and personal social services. These organisations should also be nationally based. A recent introduction has been the Opportunities for Volunteers Scheme; this only has a budget of £2 million and it is directed towards national organisations.

English Tourist Board. Under Section 4 of the Development of Tourism Act (1969) the English Tourist Board is able to make grants to tourist projects in government designated Assisted Areas. At the moment these areas are the North of England, parts of Shropshire and Northamptonshire and the extreme South West, including the Scilly Isles.

Grants or loans are only available if the recipient project fulfils the following criteria:

— attract foreign or UK tourists;
— increase tourist spending;
— create employment, either directly or indirectly;
— make a tourist's stay more enjoyable.

Although there have been one or two instances of clubs being successful most applicants for capital grants are commercial, e.g. hotels, guest houses. Clubs should take note of any development in its area as this should mean additional visitors who may like to use the club's facilities, e.g. casual golfers or squash players, especially indoor facilities if the weather is bad. Informal agreement could be negotiated with hotel owners to give details of club facilities to guests if so required.

Arts Council of Great Britain. A very small proportion of the Arts Council's budget is intended for capital projects; most is devoted to revenue grants. Sport benefits indirectly from the refurbishment of halls and other indoor facilities although these are primarily intended for the performing arts.

Countryside Commission. This is another organisation which while making grants for the improvement of facilities in the countryside makes little provision directly to voluntary organisations.

Development Commission. This was founded in 1909 and is concerned with the rural economy. Small grants are made available for interesting or imaginative schemes. Clubs will benefit more from facilities such as sports halls which are built by parish councils who receive funds from the Commission.

Water authorities. Sometimes when water authorities are developing their facilities, e.g. building new reservoirs, there may be scope for clubs to request a facility to be provided for them, either for their exclusive use or on a shared basis with the public. Clubs should be alert to the possibility and make representations at any planning enquiry.

National Council for Voluntary Organisations (a registered charity). A useful booklet which the National Council for Voluntary Organisations has produced is called *Government Grants: A Guide for Voluntary Organisations.* It publishes many other booklets which sports clubs will find of use.

Non-public sources
While much publicly funded assistance takes the form of the provision

of labour and/or materials, non-public sources will normally assist clubs by way of finance only. By giving money donors do not become involved with ordering and distributing materials, hiring equipment, paying wages, supervising staff. This would be difficult to administrate and a monetary donation is easily identifiable in the accounts.

Professional fund raising companies. A number of commercial fund raising consultants have become established to help raise finance for projects. Although clubs can consider approaching them, they should only be employed if either the project is large (over £100,000) or the time club members can give to the work connected with the project is limited. The main reasons for not using them are firstly, that they work for a fixed fee. They receive payment if successful or not. Secondly, they will want some form of advance payment. It is at the initial stage of the project that expenditure must be minimised.

Sources of aid. The following sources of finance could be approached:

— suppliers, especially breweries;
— banks for loans;
— building societies for mortgages;
— local firms;
— certain governing bodies of sport;
— charities or trusts;
— National Playing Fields Association.

Suppliers. The major supplier of goods or services to approach is a brewery, whether it is a current supplier, a prospective supplier or a competitor of the currently used brewery. The supply of alcoholic drink and additional bar goods such as mixers and crisps is very profitable and, consequently, there is much competition for this section of the market —or the free trade as it is known. For this reason, breweries are keen to assist the client, or prospective client, the club. Most clubs do change their brewery at least once so this is an accepted part of the club scene.

Brewery loans or grants are given to the club either for a specific item, such as the refurbishment of the bar and lounge or for no specified purpose. The brewery's aim is for the sale of their products to be increased and loan interest rates are linked to nominal barrels of beer sold. This calculation takes spirits, mixers, etc. into account. The rate of interest will decrease with the increase in the amount of beer sold. Usually the brewery will insist on receiving security for the loan and this can take the form of a charge on the club's property, or personal guarantees offered by members. If a charge is made on the club's property other organisations, such as the Sports Council, may ask for certain undertakings to be given by the brewery if they are to consider offering financial assistance.

Other suppliers may make a donation to the club as a gesture of goodwill, possibly as a measure of thanks for past custom or in anticipation of increased income in the future. Discounts can be "hidden" in the form of donations to the club making a large expenditure, e.g. on certain all-weather tennis courts. If a new product is being introduced into a sport or an area of the country, a club could request that a reduction in price be made on the basis that the supplier can evaluate the result of the product and players' reaction to it or the product could be demonstrated to other prospective customers.

Banks. Clearing and merchant banks can be approached for a loan for a project. A loan offer is more likely to be forthcoming if:

— the application is clearly and professionally presented;
— the club's financial affairs have been satisfactorily conducted in the past;
— the club can show that it will be able to repay any loan in addition to other commitments it may have;
— the facility is capable of being used for an alternative purpose if the club becomes bankrupt, e.g. an indoor bowls club or tennis centre is so designed that it can be converted into warehousing.

Banks will normally charge commercial rates of interest and clubs must budget both for loan repayment, as well as some capital repayment annually. Security for the loan will be needed and the foregoing comments about the problems this may cause apply here. If one bank will not offer assistance, other banks should be approached.

Building societies. In some instances a building society could be approached for a mortgage to be used towards the cost of a new facility. If a mortgage is accepted by the building society, the mortgage repayments should be included in the calculation of the club's future expenses. Security will be required either through club members' personal guarantees or as a charge on the club's property. Clubs should always approach building societies' local branch offices to see if they would consider advertising the club and its activities in a window display. Most building societies have a social policy which will allow this.

Local firms (not suppliers). If a club is going to approach firms who are not suppliers to the club, presentation is most important. Initially, a letter should be sent to a Managing Director or Chairman of a company explaining the purpose of the appeal. Care must be taken that the addressee's name and position are accurate. The letter should be concise, one side of A4 paper is the maximum and it must be typed neatly. If the club serves the needs of his company's employees or if it is able to offer a service, e.g. corporate membership or social membership, this should be stated.

The secretary of the chamber of commerce and the Rotary Club could also be requested to circulate members with details of the proposals. It should be stated that any donation will be recorded within the club's facilities, i.e. on a plaque in the club's lounge or hall. A club member should always be available to visit a firm and talk about the project. He should be supplied with plenty of information he can leave with a prospective donor—history of club, copy of plans and photograph of the area to be redeveloped. If a club is a registered charity, the advantage of covenants for tax purposes should be stressed to commercial organisations.

Governing bodies of sport. Some sports' governing bodies are able to offer financial help (as well as technical help) to their affiliated clubs. This may be in the form of grant or loan and details will be available from either the county or regional representatives or the headquarters of the sport.

Sports bodies which can offer assistance include the Lawn Tennis Association, the Rugby Football Union and the Football Association. They should be contacted before work starts and they will need to know the nature of the project, the cost (estimate should be forwarded) and details about club rules, security of tenure etc. Loan interest rates will be below commercial rates.

Charities or trusts. There are certain benefits which can accrue to a club if it receives charitable status, e.g. receipt of covenanted donations, mandatory rate relief. Clubs should also consider approaching charitable organisations and foundations who may be able to assist them with a donation towards a large project.

Some charities assist recreational projects, others youth activities and some are concerned with the welfare of inhabitants in a confined geographical location. Details of charities, their criteria and contributions are contained in the *Directory of Grant Making Trusts* which is published by the Charities Aid Foundation, available in most public libraries. Often charities are looking for worthwhile projects to support and it is for this reason that clubs should approach as many charities as possible. Charities normally have a committee structure so decisions to offer aid may take some time. Therefore, applications should be made as early as possible.

Some charities which could be approached by sports clubs include:

— Queen's Silver Jubilee Trust;
— King George V Trust;
— Variety Club of Great Britain;

— Wolfson Foundation;
— Churchill Foundation;
— Lords Taverners (especially cricket clubs);
— Butlin Fund.

National Playing Fields Association. The National Playing Fields Association, which is well-known by its initials NPFA, is a charitable organisation which aims to increase leisure opportunities for young people. In addition to its technical advice and publications, it is able to assist, among others, sports clubs with charitable status. Facilities which are also eligible for assistance are located in village halls, community centres and in women's institutes.

Loans can be offered to charitable clubs towards the acquisition of land for recreational purposes (maximum £10,000) and for outdoor playing fields, children's play equipment, changing accommodation and indoor facilities (maximum £4,000). If land is being purchased it must comply with the NPFA Model Trust Deed. Loans will be secured by personal guarantors or a willing local authority or bank.

Grants are available to voluntary clubs with charitable objectives as well as to clubs which are registered charities. The grant, to a maximum of £1,000 can be used for:

— community built play areas;
— permanent play-leadership projects;
— holiday playschemes;
— training;
— large maintenance grants;
— schemes of special merit.

The NPFA will not award grant aid to projects which have been started or are in progress unless permission for a start has been given, or to running costs, or for projects for the under 5s.

The County Playing Fields Associations can offer *loans* to voluntary sports clubs not registered as charities. The amounts available are small but interest rates are lower than those charged commercially, although they vary from county to county. Like the NPFA grants, there must be satisfactory security of tenure. Adequate insurance against fire risk to buildings must also be taken out.

All county PFAs are also able to assist the cost of children's play schemes by way of grants.

Summary
Funding Large Projects

---

1. **New major facilities have many implications**
   Questions include:
   > How will rates be altered?
   > Will overall expenditure be increased?
   > Will subscriptions be increased or will sufficient income be generated?
   > Will additional staff have to be employed?

   Although some of these will be relatively easily answered it will be a useful exercise for a club planning sub-committee to consider them. By doing this it can draw up a feasibility study with costings perhaps using a cash flow projection.

---

2. **Internal fund raising**
   Money can be raised by members' fund raising through many avenues including:
   > members' loans;
   > "100" club;
   > sale of life memberships;
   > sports events.

   Details of how to implement these activities are given with comparative advantages and disadvantages.
   Members can also do much work on a self-help basis, perhaps at cost of materials only.
   A checklist is given for promoters of events with possible problems highlighted.

---

3. **Assistance from outside sources**
   Before listing the different local and central government sources of aid there is a checklist to help all applicants. The different tiers of organisation range from the European Economic Community to the parish or town council. The appropriate government agencies are examined with special attention being given to the Sports Council, the principal grant making agency to sports clubs.

---

4. **Commercial and charitable sources**
   Increasingly there is a commercial input into developments in the sports and recreational sector and this includes voluntary sports clubs. Sources of funding now include:

101

commercial and merchant banks;
large suppliers, including breweries;
local companies.

The details which should be included on the application are given along with tips on presentation.

The assistance which is available through charities and charitable trusts is often underused and the relevant source book is mentioned. Governing bodies of sport and the National Playing Fields Association also play their part and this is detailed.

4
Sports Club Facilities

"When we build let us think we build forever."

Hopefully, when clubs develop their facilities this principle of John Ruskin will be adopted and implemented.

Floodlit football pitches, artificial ski slopes, licensed bars, line marking machines, air compressors for use by scuba divers, team minibuses—these are some of the many types of facility which sports clubs own or use.

The range of sports now played is wide and diverse. Therefore this chapter will not concentrate on individual facilities, but will look at general principles which could be followed by clubs when considering how to improve their facilities. The theoretical exercise in planning a sports club given in Appendix A will examine possible options.

Three elements which will recur continually are:

— time;
— money;
— organisation.

These ingredients will be present in the three stages of the life of a facility:

— planning a facility;
— introduction of a facility;
— maintenance and monitoring of a facility.

THE PLANNING STAGE

A development plan

A club, whether it is established, or about to be formed, should draw up an overall development plan which should allow flexibility both in the short term, e.g. 1–2 years, and the long term, 5–10 years.

This plan could include:

— the activities, i.e. sports, which will be catered for in the club and

103

the priority for introducing them if there will be more than one sport undertaken;
— the type of facilities which will be required, e.g. clubhouse, courts, pitches, floodlighting, licensed bar and the use to which they will be put;
— the area and form of accommodation needed;
— the relation between facilities—circulation within the clubhouse, position of any tennis courts and cricket areas;

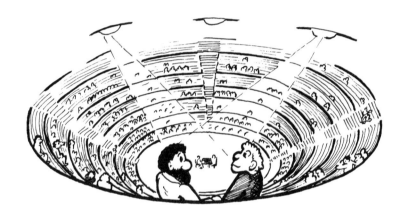

"I think he moved King to Rook Four."

— the management style to be adopted, e.g. committee structure only or committee and paid official such as club captain, manager;
— the funds available for (initial) capital investment and projected income available to meet running costs and additional capital expenditure;
— the programming of the facilities;
— requirements for the programme to allow the development plan to be completed.

The support for the development of facilities should normally be given by all members. However, in many cases the ordinary member may be reluctant to commit his time, perhaps in fund raising or even building; or money, through a possible increase in subscriptions. If this is the position an ambitious committee may have to spell out the reasons behind its progressive plans. These could include:

— the need to retain or attract new members by providing better facilities in the face of opposition from nearby clubs;
— the necessity to meet obligations imposed by league organisers concerning playing and social facilities;

— the fact that facilities have worn out, become obsolete or un-economic to maintain;

— the possibility of obtaining financial assistance in the way of grant or loan from an outside source if a facility is improved or a new facility provided.

If the membership agrees in principle that facilities should be improved a small planning group should consider the alternatives which are available. If possible this group should be led by the chairman of the overall management committee. Occupations which could make a useful contribution to the group include:

— builder;
— architect;
— surveyor;
— solicitor;
— banker;
— buyer;
— designer.

Although some projects would lead to large participation, e.g. a swimming pool, very often these are expensive to maintain and it would be wise for most clubs to go for the type of project which will generate income quickly for a club. These could include:

— sauna or solarium;
— squash courts;
— snooker room;
— indoor bowls;
— fitness room, including weight training equipment;
— floodlights;
— licensed bars (with or without catering);
— aerobics and dance classes room;
— martial arts room.

The local conditions will have to be examined, for instance the demand for squash may have been satisfied by other local providers such as private, commercial or local authority centres. Other factors to be taken into account are the possibility of growth on the site, i.e. the ability to satisfy future growth, and political constraints.

PLANNING BUILDINGS

If it is decided that a building, e.g. a new clubhouse, is required the planning committee should appoint an architect to help draw up the design. It is often a problem to know how to select an architect and the

4. SPORTS CLUB FACILITIES

Royal Institute of British Architects (RIBA) has set up a Clients' Advisory Service (CAS) which can supply information in a free leaflet which includes the regional offices of CAS. Details of architects can also be obtained from Yellow Pages, the public library, Citizen's Advice Bureau or the local authority. RIBA will also advise on scales of fees chargeable for different types of project.

The architect's role
The planning brief. The club should provide the appointed architect with a planning brief which should incorporate:

— the cost limits;
— the range of activity planned for the building;
— the pattern of use;
— the details of membership;
— the management policy;
— the residential accommodation to be included;
— the spectator facilities to be provided;
— the specialist facilities to be included.

The architect's aims. Using the brief the architect should develop a building which will be:

— suitable for its purpose;
— attractive to look at from outside and inside;
— comfortable to its users;
— durable;
— safe;
— within the club's budget and economical to maintain.

Architect's preliminary plan. This will be influenced by:

— planning considerations such as the need for certain finishes and materials and a ban on certain entertainments;
— car parking requirements;
— site restrictions such as access points, sloping land;
— a satisfactory land survey.

The relationship between club and architect. It is important for the club and architect to liaise closely and clearly. Although the club must be objective in its aims it must be flexible although it should avoid unnecessary changes in mind as this may add to architect's fees and building costs. However, it is better to change at the planning stage than when the building is under construction. The architect for his part should point out restrictions of certain facilities and try to guide the club.

4. SPORTS CLUB FACILITIES

Architect's information sources. As well as using the planning brief, an architect will use his own experience, visit other similar buildings and obtain information from relevant publications. The Sports Council's *Handbook of Sports and Recreational Building Design* and TUS Data sheets, the National Playing Fields Association's technical publications, and publications issued by governing bodies of sport such as the Lawn Tennis Association's leaflet on tennis court surfaces and the National Cricket Association's leaflet on non-turf wickets could be consulted. The architect may also consult a structural engineer, services engineer and quantity surveyor.

Architect's sketch design. The architect will produce a sketch design and this is the time for alterations. It is at this stage that the following outside organisations could be consulted about the proposals:

— the local authority's environmental health department;
— the local authority's planning department;
— the fire brigade's Fire Prevention Officer;
— the police;
— the brewery (if the club has one);
— the regional officer of the Sports Council;
— the governing body of sport.

The services engineer should have made preliminary enquiries with the suppliers of gas, electricity, oil, solid fuel, water and telephones. In some cases bodies such as British Rail or the British Waterways Board will have to be consulted if a development affects their property or activities.

Architect's scheme design. After incorporating any advice from outside bodies and taking into account any changes the club may like to make, the architect is able to produce his scheme design which will include detailed proposals for the structure and services and detailed cost estimates and equipment specifications.

It is at this stage that detailed planning permission should be obtained. Until it is received work should not start.

Architect's drawing stage and tendering. The architect will produce Bills of Quantities (with a quantity surveyor), obtain tenders and ensure that all is ready for a start on site.

Contract stage to completion of building. The architect will report regularly to the club especially if any problems arise or cost figures change. Payments will usually be made in agreed stages as work progresses. When the building is completed, the club should be given enough information to operate and maintain the building in the best manner.

4. SPORTS CLUB FACILITIES

Post contract period. It is important for the club to retain a certain proportion (normally 10 per cent) of the contract price for a period, often six or twelve months, to enable any defects in the building to be put right. During this time, the architect should help the club use the building to its maximum potential. He can also obtain feedback from the building to assist him with other projects he may undertake in the future.

Architect's timetable. A suggested timetable—which can be affected by variables such as complexities of the job, local authority, planning committee timetable, bad weather—could be:

feasibility study	— 6 months
design brief	— 2 months
sketch design	— 2 months
technical stage	— 6 months
tendering period	— 3 months
work on site	— 12 months

This period can be reduced by using standard designs of buildings, as has been seen in the Sports Council's standardised sports hall programme. Alternatively, clubs should carefully consider the option of utilising old buildings, many of which were not designed primarily for sporting purposes, e.g. old schools, churches, factories, railway stations. While work is continuing, any future employees could be appointed. It is advisable for any manager or steward to be appointed as early in the project as possible, though this will be a drain on a club's resources, so this question will have to be carefully considered.

TYPES OF SPORTS BUILDINGS

Although there are many different types of sports buildings these can be categorised into the following main groups:

— pavilions/clubhouses for seasonal sports;
— pavilions/clubhouses with many purposes with facilities for indoor games;
— specialist pavilions/clubhouses for golf, water sports;
— ancillary buildings such as scoreboxes, equipment stores.

When planning any type of building, however grand or modest a club should remember the architect's aims for a building listed above. Circulation diagrams for small and larger clubhouses and a specimen design for a clubhouse are given in Appendix A.

Cannons Club London. The spaces under disused railway arches have been imaginatively converted into this sports and social club. Note the features such as upstairs seating area, attractive bar, comfortable seating, and so on.

Building materials. Buildings may now be constructed using many types of materials—wood, brick, concrete, and in many styles—permanent constructions of brick, wood; air supported dome, prefabricated structure and of a temporary nature such as a "portacabin".

The choice a club makes is determined by many factors including:

— finance available;
— funds available for future maintenance;
— conditions laid down by the planning authority;
— constraints of the site;
— availability of public utilities;
— the possibility of expanding facilities later.

The pavilion or clubhouse.

Aspect of a pavilion. If spectator provision is to be included, pavilions should not be sited between the south west and north west

109

aspects. If this is not done spectators can be bothered by a low setting sun. The recommended angles are included in the pitch and pavilion orientation diagram produced by the National Playing Fields Association.

(Photograph by Vivian Grisogono)

Turnham Green Cricket Club, Chiswick House Park, London. This good example of a cricket pavilion incorporates essential features such as an integral scorebox and clock which are vital to the players. The committee room which is protected by shutters when not in use overlooks the pitch. To aid security a caretaker's house is attached.

If pavilions are located on exposed sites either natural or artificial protection such as "tree breaks" should be utilised.

Facilities within a pavilion. The following accommodation is likely to be found:

— changing rooms, showers and toilets;
— entrances and circulation areas, e.g. corridors;
— hall;
— club room;
— lounge;
— bar and storage area;
— kitchen;
— committee room;
— administration offices;
— first aid room;
— staff accommodation;

4. SPORTS CLUB FACILITIES

— storage areas;
— toilets.

Other facilities which are less commonly found include:

— cricket scorebox;
— squash courts;
— physiotherapy area;
— creche.

Although not being part of the building the effect of the immediate surrounding areas, i.e. patio/verandah and car park, can be important for the building itself.

Changing rooms. The required provision for different sports varies according to the nature of the game and for historical reasons. Bowls players for instance may only wish to change their shoes and a locker will be adequate. Footballers on the other hand will want to leave their clothing hanging up and will want to sit on a bench while changing. Some tennis players often have a tradition of arriving changed at the club and leaving again shortly afterwards to change at home.

As a guide, team sport players, e.g. football, hockey require 0.836 sq metre per place; bowls players 0.37 sq metre per place.

Showers and toilets should be provided for most sports and for every twelve changing spaces planned three to four showers should be built. Similarly, one WC should suffice 15–20 males (with adequate urinals), for women one WC should suit 7–10 females. Whenever possible clubs should err on the generous side, allowing for future expansion in membership or a greater use of facilities.

Clubs should not forget to plan for sex segregation of changing facilities if both sexes are using the club's facilities. Officials should have their own changing accommodation and if disabled persons or children are playing sports they will need special facilities. Changing facilities should always be separate from social facilities; this will save the embarrassment of semi-naked players walking through the hall, for example, and minimise the transfer of water and dirt between the areas.

Some sports will have special requirements, such as plunge baths for rugby players and drying off areas for sailors.

Safety, hygiene and security are essential. Extraction fans help remove steam, plastic floor coverings are more easily cleaned than wood and robust lockers keep valuables safe. Economies on hot water can be effected by installing showers which have to be worked by a hand or foot button instead of a tap and attaching the hot water supply to a time switch.

Entrances. Any entrances to the club should be welcoming and well secured. The entrance is the first part of a building that is encountered and its appearance leaves an impression on a user. It should not be cluttered and any notices should be kept to a minimum—this will stop crowding and congestion. Security should be apparent with heavy bolts and locks being a deterrent to criminals and vandals.

Certain facilities such as a shop, office, public telephone, bar or cafe could all be sited near the entrance, especially if "passing trade" is to be encouraged.

Circulation areas. These should be brightly decorated and lighted and the location for noticeboards. They can be both a barrier and link between different areas—changing, the hall, the bar and any doors leading from them should be clearly marked. If possible, corridors should have safety glass panels to allow maximum light as well as for safety and security reasons.

The hall. In many clubs it is the hall which is the focal point for social as well as sporting activities. This is especially true when the club does not have a licensed bar. A hall can be used for many purposes and activities which take place in it can bring additional income into the club. A hall can be used for the following:

— club dinners and dances;
— post match refreshments;
— jumble sales;
— indoor sports such as judo, badminton, table tennis;
— hobbies such as art classes, fly fishing lessons;
— lectures;
— pre-school playgroups;
— dance classes;
— exhibitions;
— senior citizens' clubs.

This is only a small selection of the activities for which halls through-out the country are used.

If a hall is to be used for recreational badminton it should be at least 17 m × 8.5 m × 6.7 m high. The finishes used in the hall will vary with its purposes and available funds. To allow the widest use, it should have a wooden floor with sports markings or be unmarked to accept temporary surfaces, e.g. short bowls mats, roll up badminton courts. It would be advisable for the hall:

— to be directly linked with the kitchen via a door and/or servery;
— although separated from the main body of the bar and lounge, the presence of a bar counter would allow those attending a function in the hall to be isolated from people using the lounge;
— to have access to storage space, preferably with double width doors for equipment such as chairs, tables, gymnastics equipment, mats;

— to contain recessed power sockets for loudspeakers, cleaning tools;
— to be kept as clean as possible, especially if dance classes or children are using it regularly;
— to be well lit, with variable levels of lighting if possible to cater for different events.

Club room. This room could have many uses including:

— committee meetings;
— television viewing, both recreational and coaching;
— children's room;
— quiet room for cards, chess, backgammon;
— games like snooker, space invaders.

The club rooms could be sited close to the lounge or bar so that members can take drinks to friends, wives who may be sitting there.

The lounge. The lounge is normally situated next to the bar or as part of the bar area itself. It could include the following:

— comfortable furniture—tables and chairs;
— relaxing furnishings—carpets, pictures and curtains;
— newspapers and magazines;
— a stage—preferably portable;
— background music;
— gaming machines.

The bar. It should be designed to overlook the playing area. The facilities offered in the bar can vary greatly. The club could obtain assistance from its brewery supplier in both planning the bar layout and towards the cost of fitting it out (this includes the lounge furniture and fittings). Features of the bar should include:

— good ventilation and heating;
— access to the kitchen to allow preparation of bar snacks and meals;
— direct access to the bar storage area which should have an outside door to facilitate deliveries of drink and foodstuffs;
— a well lit and spacious serving area with cash registers, optics, glass washing machines, beer pulls, bottles being well located;
— installation of a separate telephone for bar staff in case of trouble;
— close proximity to separate ladies' and gentlemen's toilets;
— good security measures such as stout lockable grilles.

The kitchen. This should be designed with hygiene and safety uppermost in mind. The kitchen should contain essential items such as:

— refrigerator;
— freezer—chest type preferably;

— cooker—gas, electric or solid fuel—with six rings and extractor fan;

— sink with hot and cold water;

— adequate food preparation surfaces (not wood);

— adequate storage areas for items like cutlery, glasses, cleaning materials;

— pest proof food storage areas;

— satisfactory waste disposal arrangements;

— suitable fire extinguishers;

— first aid kit;

— electric kettle;

— good supplies of cutlery, glasses, cooking utensils.

Optional equipment could include:

— microwave cooker (industrial type);

— waste disposal unit;

— additional freezers;

— hot plates;

— hot and cold display cabinet;

— dishwasher;

— deep fat fryer;

— washing machine;

— toasted sandwich maker.

Kitchens should be well lit and ventilated with ample space for circulation, and capable of being easily cleaned. They should be accessible to the hall and the bar serving area, with an outside exit from the clubhouse to ease deliveries.

There are several sources of information about efficient *kitchen design*. The nationalised industries like the Electricity Council and British Gas will provide a planning service for a small deposit (fee). They can be contacted through their local showrooms. There are also a number of magazines which deal with design principles and planning: the *Ideal Home Book of Kitchens* is a good example. For a detailed plan of a large scale kitchen see Richard Sprenger's *Hygiene for Management*. The local authority's environmental health department should also be consulted at the earliest opportunity as this department enforces Food Hygiene Regulations.

The committee room. If this is a separate room the only requirements are that there are good acoustics and soundproofing if possible. If it is sited near the bar this may encourage committee members to attend.

There should be a central table with sufficient chairs with a smaller table for the use of the minuting secretary. A socket for a telephone may be useful, for instance if an absent committee member has to be contacted. A lockable filing cabinet for club records and a typewriter

(Photograph by Vivian Grisogono)

Office equipment. A computer can be used, especially in larger clubs, to help with a variety of administrative tasks such as memberships, subscriptions, event results, equipment hire and court hire, as well as stock control for the bar or catering and even wages for office and other staff.

could also be kept here. As meetings sometimes take a long time some committees may not wish to allow smoking, consequently ashtrays should not be provided. Members could leave the room during a "natural break" for a smoke. Finally, a wall clock would be useful to concentrate minds.

Administrative office. If there are paid employees—bar steward, secretaries—they should be provided with working accommodation, preferably an office. This could be located near the entrance to the club where personnel would be able to supervise movements.

The offices should be well lit and ventilated to reduce eye strain, with a window if possible. There should be facilities for office machinery, a telephone and an electric kettle. Storage space will be needed, and a safe could be used for petty cash, bar takings. This could be one of the first aid locations (along with the bar, changing rooms, kitchen and groundsman's office).

4. SPORTS CLUB FACILITIES

First aid room. If a first aid room is provided, it is important that all club members know where it is located and that its location is well publicised throughout the building. If the St John's Ambulance Brigade or other medical organisations attend matches they should also be told of its location.

The room could contain:

— good lighting;
— an adjustable treatment couch;
— at least two chairs;
— a collapsible bed with clean blankets and pillows;
— access to a telephone;
— hot and cold water and towels;
— soap and disinfectant;
— moveable screens;
— resuscitation equipment;
— notices about injuries, artificial respiration;
— access to supplies of ice;
— a first aid kit;
— a stretcher kept in a cabinet.

Clubs should ensure that the room is *never* locked when an activity is taking place in the club. If a first aid room is not provided suitable alternative arrangements must be made. This subject is discussed again in Chapter Six.

Staff accommodation. Staff accommodation can be:

— located within the clubhouse;
— in a house separate from the clubhouse;
— in a caravan separate from the clubhouse.

Very often clubs will only be able to attract staff, e.g. a bar steward or groundsman, of the right calibre if they are able to offer accommodation at the club as part of the conditions of service. There are two advantages for the club in having staff living on the premises:

— a deterrent to vandalism or theft;
— the employee is always on call or easily obtainable.

If the employee lives away from the pavilion there should be a telephone extension or an outside bell attached to the clubhouse.

Storage areas. There should be at least two separate storage areas. The first would be accessible from the hall and used for tables, chairs and mats. It should have lockable double doors with recessed handles. It should have lighting and power sockets. A double width outside delivery doorway would obviate the need to carry heavy equipment through the clubhouse.

A second storage area would be used by the groundsman, mainly for outdoor maintenance equipment—tractors, mowers, paint, fertilisers —and sports equipment such as goalposts, netting. If it is sited next to the pavilion security is improved. Care must be taken over the storage of hazardous items such as petrol and chemicals and the provisions of the Health and Safety at Work Act should be observed.

Light, power and hot and cold water should be present. An outside tap will be useful especially when the groundsman's storage area is locked. A first aid kit should also be available here.

Toilets. Separate ladies' and gentlemen's toilets, WCs and urinals, should be provided in the changing accommodation and in the bar/ lounge. The provision for the changing rooms has already been given. In the bar or lounge at least two WCs for each sex and four urinals for men should be provided.

It will be necessary to provide hand basins with hot and cold water. Soap dispensers and hot air driers are more hygienic and need less maintenance than soap and towels.

Mirrors can be provided and arrangements made for the separate disposal of ladies' sanitary towels. Machines dispensing contraceptives and sanitary towels could also be provided. A secured plastic or metal waste basket of reasonable size should reduce litter. The WC cubicles should have spaces at the bottom and top of the door to allow inspection. It is not recommended that payment be requested for the use of conveniences.

Specialised facilities in a pavilion

Cricket scorebox. Often pavilions used by cricket teams will have an integral scorebox which is used to record the position of the match. Part of the front hinges up and allows the scorer(s) from each side to see the action. They are often able to adjust the runs and wickets total by mechanical means. As an alternative, helpers will periodically hang up the figures on nails. The main requirement for a scorebox is that it can accommodate two people with a table or shelf on which to rest their documents. The mechanism should work easily. If possible it should be above ground level so that the view of the occupants is not obstructed.

Squash courts. The rapid expansion in squash facilities in the 1960s and 1970s allowed many sports clubs to begin a new squash section and increase revenue. Although some squash only clubs started these were in a minority. Today future growth is in question for the dramatic increase in participation has slowed down.

Clubs wishing to build new squash courts should consult the Squash Rackets Association for technical advice. There are many types of construction of courts and technological advances have led to the introduction of the glass backed courts which allow increased spectator involvement.

4. SPORTS CLUB FACILITIES

Only if a club is sure of its market and concludes that its area still has latent demand should it proceed with a squash project. If possible, it should utilise existing facilities such as changing rooms to service the new courts. It should try to maximise the courts' revenue by encouraging off-peak use by outside bodies such as schools and local firms, as well as by encouraging its own members to attend at these times.

Sophisticated booking systems, with computerised ticketing facilities and access cards to the court are now in operation, and these should be considered in order to reduce staff time.

Physiotherapy treatment room. With the increasing interest and knowledge of sports injuries and the need to rehabilitate injured sportsmen as soon as possible, some clubs are now developing, in addition to their first aid service, a physiotherapy treatment system. As this is a very specialised subject the development of facilities will be covered in Chapter Six. If clubs do decide to develop these facilities they could consider sharing them (and the costs) with neighbouring sports clubs.

A creche. The problem of what to do with small children while parents are taking part in a sporting or social activity can be solved in some cases by the provision of a creche. This need not be an elaborate affair and can in fact be located in a room used mainly for other purposes, e.g. a clubroom or entrance area.

Most clubs should limit the length of time a child can be left to say 1½–2 hours maximum as it is difficult to arrange for a responsible person to look after children for longer than this. If women using a club can organise their own system, this will probably be a better solution. If a qualified nurse or nanny can be employed, this will ensure that mothers' worries are reduced.

Children should be confined to a certain area which is safe for them, e.g. no light switches or power sockets available. Heat should be at a maximum of 22°C but care should be taken to fix guards to radiators. Some toys should be provided and if blackboards or wall pin boards are available the children will be deterred from scribbling on ordinary wall coverings.

Mains services installation
The different choices of heating the clubhouse and methods of lighting and ventilating it should have been evaluated by the architect, structural engineer and services engineer while they were preparing the building's sketch design (see *above*).

The club should ensure that not only the capital but the building's running and repair costs have also been examined. Unless a building is being used all the time a continuous heating system is expensive and inefficient. Most systems that have to be activated when the

118

players are present will take a long time to warm the building or the area being used. One system that might be a compromise could be the installation of a Drugasar type gas heater—these do however have to be fitted to an external wall.

Clubs will find that some of their members will always want to sit on radiators—they must be dissuaded from doing this as any ensuing damage will be both expensive and inconvenient.

Items which may have to be put into the club include:

— emergency lighting (candles are one type!);
— fire and burglar alarms;
— a telephone system;
— a lighting control panel;
— facilities for television or radio broadcasts.

Specialist sports buildings

Because of the wide variety in types of specialised buildings—air domes, prefabricated buildings—and the special requirements for accommodation by some sports such as sailing or gliding, it will be necessary for clubs to obtain guidance from outside sources as to how to solve problems caused by unusual requirements. The principles of planning a building, as outlined in this chapter, should however be followed with emphasis being shifted in some cases, for example how to combat vandalism with air domes or the planning of wet and dry areas in a sailing clubhouse.

A good reference is the Sports Council's series *Handbook of Sports and Recreational Building Design* (four volumes) which deals with individual sports playing requirements and dimensions, as well as looking at all outdoor and indoor sport facilities. General principles are the same, however, and these include:

— obtaining expert advice (especially regarding shooting facilities);
— obtaining the advice and permission of the local planning department;
— safety should be uppermost in planning;
— accepting the regulations and guidance of the sport's governing body;
— tenders for the facility should be scrutinised regarding price and other factors, e.g. time and reliability of contractor;
— future possible development should be considered.

PLANNING OUTDOOR FACILITIES

Outside sports facilities can be divided into three main categories:

— general playing surfaces;

4. SPORTS CLUB FACILITIES

— specialised facilities;
— equipment.

General playing surfaces

When clubs plan their general outdoor surfaces, they will be influenced by several factors including:

— money available for capital investment;
— money available for future maintenance;
— constraints of the site;
— standard of play being catered for;
— requirements of the game.

Clubs should aim for the best surface possible with the money they have available. Items which may have to be provided in connection with a new playing surface, both natural and artificial, are:

— surface;
— sub surface;
— drainage;
— ducting for floodlights;
— fencing and access points;
— equipment and floodlights.

When clubs plan their scheme they should try to forecast future development on their site. If possible, they should aim for interruption to their programme to be reduced to a minimum. By doing this there will be little loss of income and, more importantly, players will feel that there is great continuity in their activities. One main factor which cannot be foreseen is the advance in technology which while helping some clubs will hinder others who have already installed facilities.

A playing surface should be:

— big enough to allow a sport to be played satisfactorily—standard of play may vary so the appropriate size and standard of pitch may also vary;
— approved by the governing body of sport;
— allow certain qualities such as ball spin, player/surface friction to be present within reasonable acceptable parameters;
— safe to both users and spectators;
— useable for a long period with low maintenance costs.

Artificial and natural surfaces. Many clubs now have a wide range of surfaces from which to choose. Although grass has been the traditional choice, artificial surfaces are now being increasingly introduced. This is especially true in cricket, hockey, soccer and tennis.

"Sorry lads, the batteries are going again!"

Artificial surfaces. There are two advantages artificial surfaces possess. These are greater use, especially during bad weather and if floodlighting is available; and reduced maintenance costs, they normally just have to be cleaned. The big disadvantage is the high capital cost of installation. Also, if maintenance is needed this should be carried out quickly as a small problem will quickly become a large one. Two points to be borne in mind are that chewing gum is difficult to remove from some artificial surfaces and special footwear and clothing is often required both for safety and performance improvement. One interesting article comparing the cost of natural turf and synthetic surfaces was contained in *Turf Management* (March 1983).

The variety of artificial surfaces available can often be confusing to clubs. They include:

— timber;
— artificial grass—porous, non-porous and sand filled;
— polymeric—porous and non-porous;
— mineral, e.g. asphalt;

— fibrous/felt;
— concrete.

When selecting an artificial surface, clubs should remember that a skilled contractor should be employed to do the work. The surfaces need a substrate of concrete, tarmacadam or rubber material with good drainage. As good weather is needed when the top surface is laid, clubs should not pressurise the contractor if the weather is bad.

Some governing bodies of sport, e.g. the Lawn Tennis Association, the National Cricket Association as well as the Sports Council, are able to give advice to clubs about surfaces. Clubs, when they have selected a surface, should ask the contractor to provide a list of other completed projects so that the standard of work can be assessed and past customers asked their views of the work completed.

Grass surfaces. Grass playing areas can either be seeded or turfed. Different grasses are used for different types of surfaces; a close knit grass is essential for golf putting greens while a coarser grass will be acceptable for football or rugby pitches. The length of cut gives a different surface; hockey and cricket pitches should be cut shorter than rugby pitches.

Although in some cases an existing grass area can be flattened, cut and rolled ready for use, more often however the existing surface will have to be removed, levelled and drainage carried out, good top soil added and the top surface prepared with grass and fertiliser. Although a specialist contractor is usually required very often a club member—a farmer, landscape gardener—will have the expertise to do the work satisfactorily.

It is important that the prepared grass surface is given enough time to establish itself before play starts; although this may be at least one playing season, to use the pitches too early may lead to setbacks and a great deal of additional expenditure.

For a large project an independent body such as the Sports Turf Research Institute, Bingley, Yorkshire, should be consulted. Alternatively, club members should be encouraged to use the services of the Institute of Groundsmanship who organise short courses on bowling greens, golf greenkeeping, winter games pitches renovation and maintenance. These are run mainly for their members but are open to non-members at a reasonable cost.

Although costs of playing pitches vary throughout the country, the cost guide produced by the National Playing Fields Association, which is updated regularly, should be consulted. This is however only a guide. The NPFA has also prepared technical advice on subjects such as specifications for sports ground construction (in conjunction with the Sports Turf Research Institute) and facilities for athletics. Clubs would be advised to obtain a copy of its publication list, which is available free of charge, to find suitable titles.

Sub surface and drainage. To avoid waterlogging during adverse weather, the sub surface and drainage should be given great thought. The three main considerations are:

— the necessity for a suitable outfall;
— the installation of drains;
— the methods of getting the surface water through to the drains.

As well as spiking the soil, adding sand and installing traditional clay drains, a club could instal sand slits with a stone backfill to help the water reach the drains, but this will increase the costs considerably. Most drainage schemes will require specialised equipment so again this is the job for a specialist contractor. As methods employed can vary the club should obtain tenders employing different systems. It is important that when this work is being carried out the soil is not compacted. This can be minimised by using light construction equipment.

Provision of floodlighting. If the planning authority will allow flood-lighting of a playing area it is imperative that if it is not installed at once ducting and electrical connections are installed for future use.

Different sports require different lighting levels so their governing bodies should be consulted. Other information sources are the *Lighting Guide—Sport* issued by the Chartered Institution of Building Services, and the NPFA booklet *Floodlighting of Outdoor Sports Facilities*. A club should ensure that floodlighting is insured against damage and theft.

Fencing and access points. Fencing is needed for security and the retention of balls. Clubs should ensure that the fencing is high enough, rigid and has a gap distance, whether of wooden, plastic or metal construction, which will not allow balls to pass through. Investigate maintenance costs before installing fencing.

Access points to fenced areas should not cause danger to players or their equipment, e.g. footballs, or interfere with play. They should include access which is wide enough for maintenance vehicles' use.

Pitch equipment. Some equipment such as goalposts can be fixed permanently in the ground. If possible, equipment should be remov-able with fixtures in sockets; this will allow seasonal use of the ground, allow the items to be cleaned or repaired easily and deter theft or vandalism at times when they are not in use.

Landscaping and access roads. Very often a local authority will specify details of landscaping which have to be carried out in conjunction with a building or layout project. This can often be a considerable expense and it may benefit a club to go direct to a grower rather than use a garden centre. Reduced prices can be negotiated when a bulk order is placed. Club members could also benefit if orders for their own needs are included in the order.

Children's play area and equipment. Many clubs provide facilities for children's play in the form of individual items such as a swing or in a play area with several items—climbing frame, swing, slide, roundabout. Equipment should be installed and maintained in a safe manner and sited in a position where the children can be observed and the equipment cannot easily be vandalised. Equipment should comply with British Standard 5696 and examined for any faults, such as sharp edges, upon delivery and regularly thereafter.

The National Playing Fields Association has produced a great deal of useful information; one of the most relevant publications is *Playground Management for Local Councils* which covers inspection and maintenance procedures and legal and insurance aspects. Clubs have a duty to protect children at play and they should recognise and try to prevent problems before they arise.

SPECIALIST FACILITIES

Outdoor facilities are usually thought of as grass pitches. In fact, there are a great many more types of facility which are in existence, recognised as being of a specialist nature.

These specialist facilities are varied and include:

— track and field athletics arenas;
— children's play equipment and play areas;
— cycle racing tracks;
— dinghy slipways;
— climbing walls;
— artificial ski slopes.

The best initial source of information on these types of facilities, which can be very expensive, is the relevant regional office of the Sports Council. As well as having access to technical expertise, it will have details of similar schemes in other parts of the country and knowledge of facilities which are already available and which can be used by the club—local authority facilities for instance. A club should also approach the relevant organisations listed in the section on the architect's role.

4. SPORTS CLUB FACILITIES

PROVIDING NEW EQUIPMENT

A club will need to know accurately what equipment is needed and the reasons for its provision. These reasons could include replacement of existing equipment or the need for additional equipment to improve standards or to keep up-to-date with technological changes.

Suppliers should be approached and tenders received. Factors to be taken into account when buying equipment include:

— cost of equipment;
— finance available;
— delivery dates;
— acceptance by the governing body of sport;
— cost and speed of maintenance;
— need to train members to use equipment;
— storage availability;
— safety of equipment (does it meet British Standards?);
— monopoly of supplier.

(Photograph by Vivian Grisogono)

To reduce costs some equipment can be made by club members. The illustration shows a home-made sightscreen on the left made by members of the Turnham Green Cricket Club which cost around £100, whilst the manufactured screen on the right was bought for about £500.

Information about suppliers can be gathered from talking with other clubs who have similar requirements, and by looking at advertisements

125

in newspapers or trade journals. Price stability and speed of delivery should also be taken into account when making a purchase. When negotiating with a supplier the club's officials should have a clear objective, conduct the business if possible on the club's premises and try to obtain concessions. A supplier with a new product may reduce the price if he is able to show it off at the club to other potential purchasers. This has to be weighed against the view that it is better to buy goods which have been tried and tested from a market leader, even if the cost is likely to be higher.

Hire/lease or purchase of equipment

One of the accounting tools which can be used by clubs when they are considering the alternatives of hiring or purchasing equipment is the principle of *discounted cash flow*.

The principle of discounted cash flow is influenced by the factors of inflation and interest rates. Clubs, if they did not invest their money in new facilities or purchase of stock would earn a compound interest on any funds in a bank deposit account or building society account. If for example £100 was invested for five years at 5 per cent interest the return to the club would be as follows:

Year	Capital at start of year	Interest earned during year	Capital at end of year
1	£100	£5	£105
2	£105	£5	£110
3	£110	£6	£116
4	£116	£6	£122
5	£122	£6	£128

(All figures rounded to nearest pound.)

Using these figures to calculate how much we would have to invest now to gain a future amount given the same interest (or discount rate) rate of 5 per cent, we can see that the following will give a capital value of £100 in each of the next five years:

Year in which £100 needed	Calculation	Amount to invest now at 5%	
1	N/A	£100	
2	£100/105	£95	$\frac{100}{105} \times 100$
3	£100/110	£91	$\frac{100}{110} \times 100$
4	£100/116	£86	$\frac{100}{116} \times 100$
5	£100/122	£82	$\frac{100}{122} \times 100$

4. SPORTS CLUB FACILITIES

The amounts to be invested now are the "present values" (PVs) of the future sums. The PVs are expressed as decimals shown as follows:

Year	PV factor at 5% discount
1	1
2	0.95
3	0.91
4	0.86
5	0.82

We can now work out that using a constant 5 per cent inflation rate to cover an intended expenditure of £750 four years from now (in year 5) we need to invest £750×0.82=£615 now.

A sports club can use this system to see if it would be more beneficial to buy some item or rent it. We could use as an example the cost of a tractor costing £2,000 with a life of 5 years against hiring a firm to cut the grass for this period at £500 per annum.

The easy answer is 5×£500=£2,500—more expensive than a new item by £500. Using DCF the situation is as follows, with a cost of £1,500 (£2,000−£500) in the first year. A saving of £500 is made in each subsequent year. This will be valued at:

Year	PV factor	Saving	PV saving
2	0.95	500	475 (500×0.95)
3	0.91	500	455
4	0.86	500	430
5	0.82	500	410
		Total PV	1,770

The cost of £1,500 in the first year would yield savings of £1,770 in the next four years and as a bonus the club would be left with a tractor which could be sold.

Another example would be the comparison between buying some equipment for £5,000 or purchasing in three instalments of £2,000 (again using a yearly rate of 5 per cent inflation). The three payments are worth:

Year	PV factor	Outlay	PV outlay
1	1	£2,000	£2,000
2	0.95	£2,000	£1,900
3	0.91	£2,000	£1,820
		Total PV	£5,720

The cost of £5,720 is more than one payment of £5,000—one payment should be made.

4. SPORTS CLUB FACILITIES

As a final example, if the choice is between buying a vehicle for £2,000 or renting it for £600 per annum over four years with a 5 per cent annual inflation rate, the DCF for renting option is calculated as follows:

Year	PV factor	Outlay	PV outlay
1	1	600	600
2	0.95	600	570
3	0.91	600	546
4	0.86	600	516
			2,232

Again it would be best to make one payment and purchase the vehicle.

Club officials will be pleased to learn that DCF tables are available. It is well worthwhile carrying out this exercise to gather a more accurate picture of different investment strategies.

Income and depreciation of value

Having made its decision and received the equipment, a club should ensure it is satisfactorily insured against all practicable risks. Clubs should realise that as soon as it is used it will lose value and will begin to wear and the budget should be adjusted to take these factors into account. It will be useful for the club to estimate, using discounted cash flow techniques as outlined above, what investment will be needed for future finance. Similarly, the question of whether the equipment should be hired or bought could also be investigated.

INTRODUCING A NEW FACILITY

Once a club's new facility has been completed and is about to be brought into use, its presence and availability must be advertised to present and prospective members. There are exceptions to this process; some rifle clubs for instance may not wish their new facilities to be advertised generally for fear of theft or disruption of their activities, and rely on word of mouth to obtain new members.

Publicity

Chapter Three examined the possible methods for funding a new facility. If a club sub-committee was given the task of raising the money, it may be appropriate for this group to organise the publicity with the possible addition of members with expertise in this field.

Within the club, posters should announce the news of the completion of the work and letters should be circulated to all current and past members. Special thanks should be given to those who helped, either through donating time and/or money and also to outside donors or sponsors.

Details of the facility could also be sent to the following groups, and while they may not respond directly or immediately it is likely that the benefits derived in unforeseen ways will outweigh the cost of postage:

— local authority;
— local councillors;
— local member(s) of parliament;
— regional offices of the Sports Council (and its headquarters if any financial or technical assistance was received);
— local sports council;
— local chamber of commerce;
— governing body of sport;
— the police (if appropriate);
— local newspaper—the editor and sports editor;
— local radio station—BBC or commercial;
— local schools (if appropriate);
— local library;
— clubs with whom there is strong contact;
— neighbouring firms, private individuals who may be affected;
— interested organisations such as Kidsline in London which is interested in children's facilities and activities in London.

Press conferences. If a club wishes to hold a press conference to publicise the new facility send a press release to the sports editor of the local newspaper together with the invitation to the conference. The release should be embargoed for publication until after the conference has been held. Several days notice should be given and the venue, e.g. committee room, should be large enough to hold the numbers anticipated.

The purpose is for the press to be able to ask questions. It should be kept brief and be followed by a guided tour by an officer of the club. A record should be kept of those attending and follow up telephone calls made to ascertain whether, and to what extent, a story will be published.

Copies of the press statement should be available on the day as well as additional literature which may be useful, such as reports or photographs. A wall display could be mounted which can be informative, reducing the need for copies of photographs, and available for early visitors.

The press release or statement could be in the form of an information pack including details about the facility, any press cuttings during its development and photographs, e.g. during the construction and completion phases, pictures of star players at the club and possible future visitors from opposition clubs. Club members could produce photographs, maps or sketch plans thus reducing costs.

It is unlikely that the project will be featured regionally or nationally. To help get the best results, a useful free booklet has been produced by the Central Council of Physical Recreation entitled *You and the Press*, a guide for press officers at club and county level. The CCPR has recognised the valuable support the media gives clubs and accordingly this booklet suggests many practical ways in which links can be improved.

Opening the facility
As the club should be proud of its new facility and the work which has made it possible, it should make a special attempt to show it off both to attract interest and also as a way of tangibly thanking those who have assisted. An additional aim should be to raise some money to either help club funds or possibly assist a related or local charity.

A sporting event followed by a social gathering would be the ideal but a social event may be more appropriate. Invitations should be sent out beforehand with a request for replies to facilitate catering. The invitation should include details of:

— reason for the event;
— location;
— time and date;
— dress required;
— refreshments to be provided;
— name of celebrities expected to attend.

On the day, details such as those included in tournament arrangements contained in Chapter Three should be covered. To ensure club interest in a sporting event, competitors, whether individuals or a team, should include club members. An event programme should contain details, and photographs if possible, of club players and invited celebrities, the day's schedule and background to the event and new facility.

An appropriate celebrity—a famous player, Lord Mayor, entertainer —should declare the facility open. Because of the possible interest and attendance, advertising could be solicited for the programme and coverage may be given on the television or local radio as well as in the local newspaper. Television or radio will need ample prior notice and may request certain facilities such as good parking for vans, power sockets for lighting, room to be used as a studio.

Facility signs
Before the opening of the facility the club must ensure that any

noticeboards advertising the club and its facilities are brought up-to-date. It may be useful if the board, as well as containing the details of the contact official, includes existing and projected sections and activities. These details should not be permanently affixed in case the contact alters or a sports section ceases. Hours of opening and a space for fixtures will attract visitors or spectators to the club. These signs should be displayed prominently, if possible next to a road, at a level where they can be easily seen by the maximum number of passers-by. The board should be easy to maintain, secured safely especially against high winds and be included within the club's insurance policy.

Club tel no.	Club crest	Sponsor's name/logo
	Club's name or title	

Open	M—F	hours
Open	S&S	hours

New members are welcome to play:

Bowls	Cricket	Squash
Darts	Football	Snooker
Contact	Name and position	Tel no.

ALL STANDARDS and COACHING GIVEN

Next	match on	day and time	v.
Next	match on	day and time	v.

Fig 1. Possible design for a club notice-board. The board should be prominently sited near the entrance to the clubhouse or pitches where it will generate most interest.

Clubs should also include details of new facilities in any club handbook or fixture card which is sent to other clubs or displayed in local shops or library. Members should be encouraged to do as much publicity for the new facility as possible.

MAINTENANCE AND MONITORING

Most new projects have teething troubles; hopefully most will be corrected with a minimum of fuss. It is during this six or twelve month period, that the amount of retention money kept by the club acts to ease anxieties and ensure problems are rectified. While most contractors are reputable, there will be exceptions to this situation.

Members should be encouraged to report faults to the officer detailed for this job and a record kept. The architect must be kept informed of the situation and if any serious problems occur he should be asked for advice.

The most likely alterations needed will be in the programming of the facility; anticipated use by a certain group or at a certain time may not materialise and if this happens an alternative use should be implemented if possible; for example an under used squash court could be the location for weight training equipment (with the floor surface suitably protected).

The club should budget for redecoration or renewal after a time. The need to redecorate the bar and changing rooms will normally be greater than the need to redecorate the scorebox or committee room. Sometimes assistance can be obtained towards the cost of improving the bar and lounge from the brewery supplier.

Users should be asked regularly, either formally or informally, about the facility and what could be changed, improved, replaced. Club officials should be sensitive to changes in members' views at all times and if changes are impracticable for financial or other reasons, the proposer should be given the reason and not left to speculate why his valuable assistance to the running of the club's affairs has been rejected.

Summary

Club Facilities

1. **Planning a new facility**
   Three key elements clubs should take into account when
   thinking about a new facility are—time, money and organisation.
   These are important in the three phases of a development,
   namely:
   >   planning stage;
   >   introduction of a facility;
   >   maintenance and monitoring.

2. **A development plan**
   A sub-committee should draw up a club development plan for
   the short and long terms. These should consider the club's needs
   in respect of:
   >   activities;
   >   facilities required;
   >   management style;
   >   funding.

3. **Club's relationship with an architect**
   If an architect (or other expert) is engaged he will liaise closely
   with the planning committee at the following stages (this process
   applies to new buildings and to conversion work):
   >   feasibility study;
   >   design brief;
   >   sketch design;
   >   technical stage;
   >   tendering period;
   >   work on site.
   A timescale is suggested as a guide only.

4. **Types of sports building**
   The many types of sports building can be categorised as follows:
   >   pavilions for seasonal sports;
   >   multi purpose pavilions;

specialist pavilions;
ancillary buildings.
Factors associated with sports buildings to be considered:
type of structure—permanent, air dome, temporary;
aspect of pavilion;
facilities included.

5. Facilities within the building

There are many possible facilities which can be included within
a clubhouse. These are listed individually with specific
locations and a list of requirements:
the hall;
changing areas;
lounge;
bar;
storage areas;
committee room.
Some specialist facilities are also discussed, including:
scorebox;
squash courts;
physiotherapy room;
creche.

6. Outdoor facilities

These are divided into general playing surfaces, specialist
facilities and equipment.
General planning policies are examined including the subject of
artificial and natural surfaces.
A few examples of specialist facilities are listed but the best
approach for clubs is to contact outside advisors who will have
knowledge of comparable projects.

7. New equipment

Factors influencing the purchase of equipment include its cost,
finance available, maintenance, safety and delivery dates. A
comparison is made between leasing and purchase and a method
whereby a club can calculate how much it will have to save to
replace equipment.

8. Introduction of a facility

Publicity and press conferences to announce a new facility and an opening event are listed and a design for a club noticeboard aimed at attracting new members is shown.

---

9. Maintenance and monitoring a new facility
General points are made about the need to monitor a new facility, especially taking into account members' views.

5
Sports Clubs and the Law

"Government and co-operation in all things are the laws of life; anarchy and competition the laws of death."

The good sense of John Ruskin's words is clearly demonstrated in the relationship between a club and the law. Chapter One showed that the form sports clubs can take is very varied and, as such, different types of club are subject to different legislation, although certain laws and legal precedents apply generally. Knowledge of this field is of special importance to club officials who may be liable, at any moment, to be sued. Penalties exist if they are successfully prosecuted for whatever reason.

As the subject of law is most complicated, and expensive to negotiate, clubs would be well advised to have access to legal advice whether from a solicitor, barrister or consultant within the club's membership, or employed on the club's behalf from outside.

Legislation applies to specific aspects of a club's operation including:

— planning and building a new facility;
— the bar and catering services;
— employment of staff;
— safety within the club;
— behaviour of members (on and off the playing area);
— insurances;
— revenue raising;
— responsibilities of club officials;
— formation of clubs.

PLANNING AND BUILDING

Because of the pressure on space in this country, a sophisticated planning system has developed to control new buildings, major alterations and enlargements to existing buildings, and the change in use of buildings and land. Permission is needed, for instance, to build a large new pavilion, erect floodlights etc. While some changes such

136

as from a grass tennis court to an all-weather surfaced court may not need permission, this is indeed the case in some instances. The planning process which is the responsibility of local authorities under the Town and Country Planning Act 1971 allows for consultations with public authorities and people, such as neighbours, who might be affected by an application.

A club should contact the planning department of the local authority at the earliest possible opportunity to discuss its proposed scheme. There are two types of planning permission for a project—outline and conditional (or detailed). Outline permission gives acceptance in principle for a new pavilion, floodlights etc. to be built. When full permission is granted this is subject to certain conditions, which can include the stipulation of use of certain materials or restrictions on the period of use of the facility.

Normally an application is considered within eight weeks. In most instances, the decision is made by the local authority's planning committee although in some cases it may be delegated to the chief officer responsible for planning.

If the application is refused an appeal can be lodged with the Secretary of State for the Environment. The development control section of the planning department will advise an applicant how to appeal, and will also advise about appeals against an enforcement notice which is issued by the local authority when a club starts work on a project when detailed planning permission is not forthcoming.

It is unlikely that a club will be considered for financial assistance towards a building project by bodies such as the Sports Council or National Playing Fields Association unless detailed planning permission has been granted.

Usually approval under the building regulations will be needed when planning permission for a development is required. Sometimes, however, when a development is quite small, planning permission is not required but building regulations approval may still be necessary.

Unfortunately, there is a cost for both planning permission and building regulations approval and the cost increases with the complexity of the project. The planning department will advise on amounts.

If a club wishes to develop its facilities and is refused permission to do so, it should appeal against the decision; even if the inspector at the ensuing public enquiry rules against the club he may recommend another application be submitted with the facility being positioned differently.

The Royal Town Planning Institute (RTPI) issues a useful booklet Where to Find Planning Advice which explains concisely the planning system and contains a list of planning consultants including those who handle leisure projects. The RTPI also issues a further three useful free leaflets: Your Planning Application, Should I Appeal?, Can I Object?

A club should be aware of any proposed development which may affect its activities; for instance if a house is to be built next to a cricket ground there may be possible problems at a later stage with cricket balls being hit through windows. If necessary, objections to the application should be lodged.

If a club's application is complicated, or if it encounters problems, fees paid to a planning consultant will be money well spent.

Fire precautions
Unless the club is planning a stadium catering for over 10,000 people, it will fall outside the scope of the Fire Prevention Act 1971. However, if there is a workplace contained within the proposed development, e.g. a secretary's office, the fire brigade will become involved especially with the siting of fire exits. It is advisable for a club to consult with the Fire Prevention Officer at an early stage of planning.

Control of Pollution Act 1974
Although this is a wide ranging act dealing with most forms of environmental pollution, e.g. smoke, smells and noise, it is the last of these which is most relevant to sports club activities.

Local authorities are able to stipulate the permitted noise level while a building is being constructed. It can impose noise emission levels once the new facility is in use. Also under the Act, individuals are able to go to a magistrate's court to complain about noise nuisance. If a club stages many noisy functions its neighbours could invoke this clause and it may be taken into consideration when a club's registration certificate is being renewed.

Access for the disabled
With the greater involvement of disabled people in society and its activities, including sport, there has been a greater awareness of their problems especially with regard to access to facilities. When planning their new facilities, clubs should have regard to the needs of the disabled and take care over items such as access and egress and notices within buildings. Although a new ramp for wheelchair use may increase building costs, this will open up the facility to a new sector of society. Incidentally this ramp could also be used by ladies pushing prams and buggies on their way to a post-natal aerobics class. Clubs should also take note of the provisions of the Chronically Sick and Disabled Persons Act 1970.

THE BAR AND CATERING SERVICES

Chapters Two and Three showed that the licensed bar and catering services can make an important contribution to a club's finances. It is essential that this income is not lost to the club through transgression of licensing laws.

The bar

Liquor licences. The Licensing Act 1964 regulates the sale or supply of alcohol. It is preferable for a club to be licensed under Part II of this Act and obtain a *registration certificate*. This has several advantages over a justice's licence including:

— the police do not have as wide rights of entry into registered clubs as licensed premises;
— local publicans are unable to object to the issue of a certificate as a matter of course;
— the period of a registration certificate is longer than an annual licence;
— justices do not have sole discretion to refuse a registration certificate unlike their powers in connection with a licence.

The application for a certificate has to be made to the clerk of the magistrate's court covering the area in which the club is situated. It must be signed by the club chairman or secretary and be advertised in the club and in a local newspaper.

There are criteria which the club has to satisfy to become registered and these include having at least twenty-five members and an interval of at least two days between a membership application and the right to enjoy the privileges of membership.

There are grounds for objection by the police, the local authority or occupier of other premises on renewal. These are:

— the club is not qualified for registration;
— the premises have been disqualified for use as a club;
— the application is incomplete or inaccurate or does not comply with the Act;
— the premises are not suitable (because of size, condition or nature of the club).

If any of these are proved the magistrates have to refuse an application. Discretionary grounds of objection include:

— the club being conducted in a disorderly manner;
— in the previous year there have been illegal sales of alcohol;
— club premises are habitually used for an unlawful purpose.

Once a club has been granted a certificate it must be careful not to abuse the situation as the certificate will be cancelled for certain reasons, although the club is able to appeal in the crown court against refusal of renewal or cancellation of a certificate.

Clubs should ensure that any changes in their rules are notified to the police and local authority within twenty-eight days; club officers may be liable to prosecution if this is not done.

Renewal applications are also made to the magistrates court.

Clubs can alternatively apply for a *liquor licence* to the licensing justice of the local area. There are five types of licence:

— all intoxicating liquor;
— beer, cider and wine:
— beer and cider only;
— cider only;
— wine only.

Any licence is valid only for one year and one club officer has to bear the responsibility of being the "licensee". This means that he incurs criminal liability for any infringement of the Act.

Clubs, whether licensed or having a registration certificate, can apply for an *extension to normal bar hours* associated with the supply of needs, or through an exemption order for a special occasion such as a tournament or social event. Applications should be made in advance with, if possible, twenty-eight days' notice being given.

The club's rules on *sale of alcohol to non-members* should be clear. If they stipulate that only club members may purchase drinks, it may be argued that if guests purchase drinks it is likely that the sale will be held as illegal. If the rules do not say this, then it is likely that guests and members are viewed similarly concerning the sale of alcohol.

If an outside group hires the club or a member invites his guests to a private function, such as a 21st birthday party, those guests are classified as visitors. They are allowed to purchase alcohol under the Act. Clubs should be careful not to abuse this facility otherwise the magistrates may feel the club is not being conducted in good faith, and either refuse or modify the club's registration certificate.

If a club has a registration certificate it is able, if club rules allow it, to *sell alcohol to people under 18*. Again, a club must ensure it is being run in a "bona fide" manner with no danger of its certificate being withdrawn or modified. A club can also employ people under 18 to serve behind the bar. If a club decides to sell alcohol to those under 18, it would perhaps be wise for them to be served only with beer and lager.

If a club does not have a licensed bar it can obtain an *occasional licence* under the Act for special events. This is obtained through an existing licensee (local publican or off-licence manager) who will give his permission to run a bar at the club for the event—normally in return for being able to supply the drinks.

5. SPORTS CLUBS AND THE LAW

Catering services

Sports clubs' catering operations vary from selling snacks and rolls in the bar, to preparing post-match refreshment for players and spectators, to restaurant-type meals service with many other variations. Clubs are liable to legislation about food and these are contained in:

— Acts of Parliament;
— Regulations made by an appropriate minister;
— Acts or by-laws made by local authorities.

Copies of these Acts and Regulations can be obtained from Her Majesty's Stationery Office. The Regulations are known as Statutory Instruments and have numbers for reference purposes.

The appropriate department of the local authority with responsibility for catering matters is the environmental health department. Qualified officers have wide powers including entry to premises at all reasonable hours to obtain samples and seize unfit food. Clubs would be advised when planning or altering a catering facility to consult, at the earliest possible opportunity, the environmental health department. Legislation which may affect clubs is:

— Food and Drugs Act 1955;
— Food and Drugs (Control of Food Premises) Act 1976;
— Food and Drugs (Amendment) Act 1982;
— The Food Hygiene (General) Regulations 1970.

The Food Hygiene (General) Regulations 1970. These Regulations are aimed at avoiding food poisoning and cover the following subjects:

— premises;
— equipment;
— food handlers;
— washing facilities;
— services;
— practices.

Premises. These must be maintained in a clean condition with food rooms having satisfactory standards of lighting and ventilation and being constructed of materials which can be easily cleaned. Pests should not be able to enter. Refuse must be conveniently disposed of.

Equipment. Equipment must be kept clean and be made of non-absorbent material.

Food handlers. Food handlers must be clean and those suffering from food poisoning or disease must not be allowed to handle food. Spitting and use of tobacco is prohibited.

Washing facilities. Hand basins, soap, nailbrushes and drying facilities must be provided for food handlers. Washing facilities for food and equipment must be fitted with hot and cold water.

Services. There must be an adequate, clean and wholesome supply of water. Drainage systems must not ventilate into food rooms. Sanitary conveniences must not be used for handling food. Suitable first aid materials, including waterproof dressings, must be provided.

Practices. These include unfit and fit food being separated before sale. Food must not be placed lower than 45 centimetres from the ground and high-risk foods must be kept below 10°C or above 63°C.

Clubs which are guilty of contravening the Regulations may be very heavily fined for each offence.

The Health and Safety at Work Act 1974. Although this Act applies to all areas of activity within the club, it is perhaps most widely applicable within the bar and catering areas. The Act is enforced by an inspectorate working under the direction of the Health and Safety Executive and by local authority environmental health officers.

The Act has three main objectives:

1. To secure the health, safety and welfare of persons at work.
2. To protect non-employees and members of the public against risks to health and safety arising from the activities of persons at work.
3. To control the keeping and use of dangerous substances.

The Act encourages management to promote health and safety, including the supervision and training of staff. Most employers must prepare and revise a written safety policy and bring this to the attention of their staff, but if there are less than six employees this is not necessary. The Health and Safety Executive has issued guidance notes on policy standards for employers and this is available from its headquarters or area offices. Each area office has an inspector who is responsible for entertainments and sports grounds who will advise clubs. If an inspector, who has powers to enter club premises at a reasonable time, feels the Act is being contravened he can give advice verbally or in writing or he can issue an "improvement notice". Finally if the activities may cause serious injury he can issue a "prohibition notice". Failure to comply with a "prohibition notice" may lead to prosecution. A club is able to appeal against the issue of these notices to an industrial tribunal.

Weights and measures. Clubs should be sure that the measures given when serving drinks are within accepted levels. Customs and Excise officers are able to make spot checks and if measures are short the club is liable to prosecution.

EMPLOYMENT OF STAFF

Clubs are affected by legislation concerning the selection and the conditions attached to the employment of paid staff. These include:

— Equal Pay Act 1970;
— Sex Discrimination Act 1975;
— Race Relations Act 1976;
— Employment Protection Act 1975.

Equal Pay Act 1970

This was introduced to eliminate or diminish discrimination between the sexes regarding pay and other terms of contract. The Act covers full time and part time employees.

The Act applies as long as the work of men and women is the same or very similar. There are some exceptions and these include any special treatment connected with the birth of a child.

If a club contravenes the Act and a complaint is upheld by an industrial tribunal it can be ordered to pay compensation.

Sex Discrimination Act 1975

The provisions of this Act only apply to clubs who employ at least six people (including part time employees).

If the Act is applicable to the club it is unlawful to discriminate on sex grounds against a man or woman and the provisions apply to recruitment, promotion and benefits etc.

It is interesting that a single sex member club is allowed but this situation should be examined closely for various reasons as pointed out in Chapter One.

Race Relations Act 1976

It is unlawful for a club as an employer to discriminate against a person of a particular racial group on the grounds of his colour, race, nationality or ethnic or national origins. All clubs are subject to the provisions of this Act.

Clubs are also liable under this Act when considering applicants for membership.

If a club is found guilty of contravening the Act it can be ordered to pay compensation by a county court or sheriff's court.

Employment Protection Act 1975

This Act gives employees certain rights including:

— guaranteed payment, after four weeks, if the employer is unable to provide work;
— maternity rights for expectant mothers;
— rights for time off work either paid or unpaid for certain reasons;
— written statement of dismissal and an itemised pay statement for employees.

The actual method of payment of staff is also guarded by legislation such as the Truck Acts 1831 to 1940, and requirements imposed by the Inland Revenue, Department of Health and Social Security and the Wages Councils.

The Inland Revenue
The Revenue imposes a duty on the club to deduct income tax under the PAYE system from any employee. Because of the complexities of the system and the documentation needed to operate it, clubs would be advised to obtain a copy of the booklet *The Employers' Guide to PAYE* which is available from a local tax office.

It may be easier from the club's point of view to employ staff who are self employed, so that they are fully responsible for taxation and national insurance contributions and the club simply pays a gross amount without deductions.

National Insurance
Staff who are employed by a club under a contract have to pay Class 1 contributions. Clubs would be advised to obtain the following free booklets which are produced by the DHSS:

— Employers' Guide to National Insurance Contributions (NP15);
— Class 1 contribution rates (NP28);
— National Insurance contribution rates (NI208);
— National Insurance Contract of Service (NI39).

Self-employed staff would be responsible for their own National Insurance contributions.

Wages Councils
Most staff employed by a club are covered by one of two Wages Council orders. The Councils were established under the Wages Council Act 1959. The orders set minimum wages and conditions of employment such as leave entitlement. They do not cover green-keepers, groundsmen or gardeners.

Copies of the orders covering club stewards (LNR(160)) and bar staff (LNR(159)) can be obtained from the Office of Wages Councils. These two notices must be posted prominently in the club.

SAFETY WITHIN AND OUTSIDE THE CLUB

In sport very often the irresistible force meets the immovable object and the result can be disastrous. The force which is exerted in sporting events, whether it is the weight of a galloping horse, the speed of an ice hockey puck or the velocity of a rifle bullet, has to be controlled and contained as far as possible.

To this end, there is a duty owed by occupiers of premises, whether a club committee, promoter or company for the safety of visitors in all circumstances who come onto their property. This is a statutory liability under the Unfair Contract Terms Act 1977.

Another piece of legislation which deals with this subject is the Defective Premises Act 1972. Although sports stadia which are designed to hold more than 10,000 people are subject to the provisions of the Safety of Sports Grounds Act 1975, most sports club facilities will not be on this scale and therefore incidents which occur will be influenced by case law which has developed, mainly within the last century.

Judicial decisions have been given in favour of victims of collapsed grandstands at Blackburn[1] and Cheltenham[2] (for references see Appendix G) where the organisers failed to exercise proper care. Decisions in favour of the promoters of sports events, because there had been no lack of safety, were given over incidents at Haringay ice hockey, where a rink-side spectator was hit by a puck,[3] and at the White City horse show where a photographer was injured by a horse.[4]

Basically, these results show the difference between consenting to the normal risks of sporting events (such as the spectator at Haringay and the photographer at the White City) and where no such consent occurs or can be inferred, e.g. at Blackburn or Cheltenham, for negligent construction of spectator facilities.

Many sports clubs run into difficulties when the results of their activities adversely affect their neighbours. The most frequent of these are the instances of golfballs, cricket balls and footballs being hit into adjacent properties. Liability can give rise to damages and/or injunctions or both. Injunctions, however, are always discretionary and vary according to the circumstances of a particular case which can often be finely and delicately balanced to create apparently contrasting and conflicting judicial decisions.

The best defence a club can put forward to claims against it is that it has taken all reasonable precautions against this eventuality, such as altering the line of a cricket wicket or erecting protective netting. Furthermore, in certain circumstances it could argue upon the appropriate fact that a complainant has consented or acquiesced in a grievance by accepting it or appearing to have acted with knowledge of it, e.g. by purchasing with an awareness of likely difficulties, such as premises adjoining noisy sporting areas.

BEHAVIOUR OF MEMBERS

This can be looked at as the actions of members as players on the field and their actions away from the playing field.

On the pitch
On the playing field or court it is important that participants obey the laws of their sport. If there is intent to transgress the rules then if there are serious consequences, such as injury or more rarely death, it is possible for a criminal prosecution and a claim for damages to follow. This situation has occurred after a broken leg caused by separate reckless or foul play during football matches in Sussex[5] and Cornwall[6] and a broken jaw caused by a foul rugby tackle in South Wales[7] (for references see Appendix G).

Players should realise that if they transgress the rules and consequently hurt a spectator or member of public they are liable for prosecution or a claim for damages for personal injury.[8]

In the clubhouse
Just because individuals become part of the club "family" in their own clubhouse, other clubhouses, and travelling to events and fixtures this does not allow them any rights to break the law, whether civil or criminal. Success at a tournament or on tour does not excuse a team wrecking a hotel suite or stealing any item, no matter how bizarre. Similarly high jinks in the bar can prove costly if a member's

suit is ruined by having drink or food thrown over it or if his chair is pulled from under him causing damage to his back.

Members should show regard for neighbours when carrying out their activities. Noise nuisance must be minimised, for example, by leaving a club in an orderly manner at the end of a disco or other late night event.

INSURANCES

Prudent clubs should work out the insurances they need to take out; some types are necessary and others are optional. Those which are *necessary* are:

— employers' liability;
— public liability;
— premises, e.g. buildings;
— property and income.

Those which are *optional* include:

— players' insurance;
— specific event insurance, e.g. against rain;
— foreign travel.

Necessary insurance

Employers' liability. If a club has any employees, under the Employers' Liability Compulsory Insurance Act 1969, it must insure against them being injured at work through negligence of any other employee or of the club itself. The premium is calculated on a percentage of the total wages and salaries paid and the insurance certificate must be displayed prominently in the club.

Public liability. This covers claims from members of the public against the club for damage in respect of accidents on the club's premises. The insurance should cover liability when the club's facilities are used by other groups or for unusual purposes such as open air fêtes. When a club is hiring out its facilities, it should include the insurance cost as part of the rental charged.

Premises insurance. Premises whether they are buildings such as clubhouses, pavilions, store rooms and scoreboxes, or playing facilities such as floodlights or netting around tennis courts or artificial cricket wickets, should be covered against any hazard, e.g. fire, vandalism or theft. (Insurance policies have been arranged by the National Cricket Association.)

Insurance cover should be updated regularly to take into account inflation and should include an additional small element to cover possible professional fees which may be incurred if a new building or facility has to be provided.

Clubs will find that grant-making bodies will require the club to have full insurance cover.

Property and income. All the property owned by a club, including goods in transit and cups won and held by other clubs, should be insured if possible for their replacement value. If a theft occurs and income is lost by the club this too can be insured against.

Optional insurances

Players' insurance. Clubs can either insure their players' equipment or health or draw members' attention to the advantages of taking out their own insurance. The governing body of sport should be contacted regarding its own insurance or advantageous terms for its members because of the numbers involved. Some of the private health schemes have group memberships which could be investigated. MILAS Sportsplan Insurance Policy, for example, provides benefit for personal accident, personal liability, physiotherapy fees and loss of sports equipment.

As a word of caution, the biggest deficiency in health insurance cover is that dealing with dental care. As damage to teeth and gums is one of the most common types of accident in sports such as hockey and rugby, this area should be examined when considering health insurance.

Foreign travel. If a club is travelling abroad, insurance should be taken out, especially to cover medical costs.

Specific event insurance. Clubs could consider taking out insurance cover against certain risks, especially adverse weather, when planning an event.

Insurance premiums

Insurance premiums will rise when the value of a club's property and facilities is increased, whether by inflation or addition/replacement. It is essential for a club to insure against any loss it could not afford to incur, as well as taking out public and employer's liability policies.

REVENUE RAISING

Although clubs may be enthusiastic in their efforts to raise funds to help finance day-to-day running costs, or the provision of new facilities, they should remember that their activities are closely regulated. Regulations governing this area are contained in:

5. SPORTS CLUBS AND THE LAW

— The Licensing Act 1964;
— The Gaming Act 1968;
— The Lotteries and Amusements Act 1976;
— The Betting and Gaming Duties Act 1972;
— The Local Government (Miscellaneous Provisions) Act 1976;
— The Local Government Act 1972;
— The Physical Training and Recreation Act 1937;
— The Greater London Council General Powers Act 1970.

The Licensing Act 1964

In Chapter Two, and earlier in this chapter, how clubs can apply for either a registration certificate or a licence under this Act was discussed. The Act sets out the procedures for application, the possible conditions attached to the certificate or licence, how it is renewed and how objections can be lodged. The day-to-day matters of licensing hours, sale of alcohol to guests and visitors to the club and position concerning those under 18 are also dealt with by the Act's provisions.

The Gaming Act 1968

This covers the conditions relating to registration and fees for machines such as "one armed bandits". Sports clubs will find most benefit by registering under Part III of the Act. Applications for a licence are considered by the Licensing Justices and the procedures for applying can be ascertained at a magistrates court. Most clubs will be in premises which have not received local authority approval—this situation is more appropriate to other types of premises, such as shops and taxi offices, which have a machine for their customers' use.

The Lotteries and Amusement Act 1976

Any type of raffle organised in a club is a lottery, unless those taking part use skill or judgement in the competition. These lotteries can be on a large scale, or very small held in the bar after the match. If the lottery derives revenue from non-club members it comes under the control of the local authority. If members only take part, it does not do so.

There are three types of lottery:

— the Society's lottery;
— the Private lottery;
— the Small lottery.

The Society's Lottery (under Section 5 of the Act). All money raised must be used by the sports club and no private gain can be made. There are certain conditions which have to be met including:

1. The club must be registered with the local authority.

2. The value of tickets sold must be less than £5,000. Above £5,000, the lottery has to be registered with the Gaming Board.
3. After the lottery has been held relevant details must be submitted to the local authority including prizes and expenses items.
4. Only an authorised club member can promote the lottery.
5. No prize can exceed £1,000 out of a total of £5,000.
6. Expenses are limited to a maximum of 25 per cent if the lottery does not exceed £5,000.
7. No ticket can be sold to or by a person under 16.
8. No ticket can be sold in the street except from a kiosk; its price cannot exceed 25p.
9. All tickets must specify the name of the club, the promoter's name and address and date of the lottery.

The Private Lottery (under Section 4 of the Act). This is a lottery conducted among club members and its conditions include:

1. Only a club member, authorised by the committee, can be the promoter.
2. The lottery can only be advertised on club property and on the ticket.
3. After paying printing expenses all proceeds must be given to the club.
4. Only the person who bought a winning ticket will be presented with a prize.

The Small Lottery (under Section 3 of the Act). This is the most common type of lottery and is usually part of a larger entertainment such as a dance, tournament or dinner. Its conditions include:

1. No money prizes shall be offered.
2. Tickets will only be sold and the draw take place at the entertainment's location and while it takes place.

The Betting and Gaming Duties Acts 1972 and 1981
These Acts together with the Gaming Act and Lotteries Act allow bingo to be played at a club.

The Local Government (Miscellaneous Provisions) Act 1976
Section 19 of the Act gives local authorities the powers to make a grant or loan to any voluntary organisation providing recreational facilities.

The Local Government Act 1972
Section 137 of the Act allows local authorities to make a grant to a club. This can be the product of up to 2p in the £ rate. Fine examples

of this Act being utilised can be seen at the Huntingdon indoor bowls club and gymnastics centre which were grant aided by the Huntingdon Town Council.

The Physical Training and Recreation Act 1937
This Act is the basis of the Sports Council's ability to make grants to sports clubs. Its actual funds are voted to it annually by the Department of the Environment.

The Greater London Council General Powers Act 1970
Section 14 of this Act allows the GLC to make grants to voluntary clubs within its administrative area. At the time of writing it is not clear whether the council will be abolished, and if it is whether borough councils will be given additional powers or funds to take over its role.

Dancing, music and singing licences
If a club's facilities are used for dancing or music, e.g. an aerobics class organised by outside persons, it is likely that a licence will be needed. The club should check with the local authority. Conditions of a licence for a "public place of entertainment" vary throughout the country and clubs have to comply with conditions contained in statutory regulations, and with certain by-laws.

RESPONSIBILITIES OF CLUB OFFICIALS

Officials, the committee and trustees of ordinary unincorporated sports clubs should be aware that they and not the club will be liable under law if the club is sued, as the club has no legal identity of its own. This principle was stated in the last century when the committee of Blackburn Rovers Football Club, who had employed an incompetent contractor to repair a stand, was sued when the stand collapsed and injured spectators. It is to minimise this risk of officials being sued which may influence clubs to become incorporated as companies or registered as a Friendly Society or under the Industrial and Provident Societies Act.

Club secretaries have a responsibility not to exceed their own powers and if they do this by incurring unauthorised obligations beyond those indicated in the club's Rules and Articles of Association they can be held liable.

FORMATION OF CLUBS

Chapter One explained how clubs could be formed and managed in different ways. It is useful to reiterate the legislation which deals with club formation:

Private members' clubs—no specific Acts.

Private members' clubs with trustees—many, especially the Trustees Act 1925.

Clubs as limited companies with shares—governed by the Companies Acts.

Clubs as limited companies with guarantees—governed by the Companies Acts.

Members' clubs combined with a limited company—the subsidiary limited company is governed by the Companies Acts.

Clubs formed as charities—governed by the Charities Act 1960 and Recreational Charities Act 1958.

Clubs can be registered under the Friendly Societies Act 1974.

Clubs can be registered under the Industrial and Provident Societies Acts 1965 and 1968.

Summary

Sports Clubs and the Law

1. Legislation as applicable to sports clubs
Legislation applies to sports clubs as it does to other types of organisation. It is easily identified in many fields, including:
> planning and building a new facility;
> the bar and kitchen;
> employment of staff;
> safety;
> formation of clubs;
> raising revenue.

The various acts and other legislation are described so too are the methods of making applications, e.g. for licences.

2. Organisations which apply the law
The roles and duties of organisations, such as the Inland Revenue and the Wages Councils, are explained and the relevant explanatory leaflets which may assist club officials are listed.

3. Legal precedents
The various cases in the sporting world which have been seen as precedents are mentioned and a background to the judgements is given. As these are as relevant today they will be of great assistance to clubs and officers who may be personally liable.

6
Coaching, Accidents, Injuries

"25 per cent of the football injuries were due to fouls. Enforcement of the rules is a must."

U. Jørgensen on Norwegian Association Football

The desire to learn or improve a skill or technique is one of the reasons why people play sport. Sports clubs offer the coaching facilities necessary for this learning process.

The sports club has a duty in law to safeguard, as far as is practicable, the health and safety of its employees, besides its duty to provide and maintain facilities and activities conforming to the highest standards of safety for its members and visitors. Accordingly, the risk of injuries and accidents both on and off the playing field should be minimised. When an accident happens, prompt and appropriate action should be taken. Some guidelines on providing adequate coaching facilities and medical cover in case of accidents will be contained in this chapter.

COACHING

Players learn the skills and laws of their game in their sports clubs. At the recreational level, parent teaches child, husband teaches wife and vice versa; at elite competitive level, the national coach teaches the top performers. The coach aims to help the player fulfil his aspirations, whether these comprise enjoying a game for its own sake, or trying to win top-class competitions.

Any coach, at any level, should be able to teach the following basic factors common to all sports:

— technique;
— fitness training appropriate to the sport;
— tactics;
— enthusiasm.

Even in a team sport, the coach should be able to apply individual correction to particular faults.

(Courtesy the Sports Council)

Coaching beginners in fencing. Note the emphasis on safety: the heavy duty nylon/cotton protective half-jackets, non-slip shoes, face fasks, long trousers, glove for leading hand, button on end of foil blade. The full jacket worn by the instructor is increasingly used at this level, and is standard at higher levels.

In order to teach a sport efficiently, a coach *must* have the following characteristics:

— the ability to communicate with individuals or groups;
— a certain amount of technical expertise in the sport (although the best players do not necessarily make the best coaches);
— an ability to analyse skills;
— an understanding of the sport;
— an understanding of body mechanics.

The coach who studies his subject deeply, or who takes a coaching qualification, will gain an increased and more scientific awareness of physiology (how the body works), psychology (how the mind works), and the prevention and immediate treatment of injuries.

Qualifications
Within clubs, members who are players, ex-players or enthusiasts often provide a valuable service in teaching beginners and children their sport. They pass on their knowledge and experience.

Most governing bodies of sports organise coaching courses designed to teach and further coaching skills. The courses are usually organised in grades, from elementary amateur to top-level professional. Certificates are normally awarded to define what level the trainee coach has reached. Details of the courses are available from the relevant governing body.

Clubs should encourage members who wish to teach their sport to undertake coaches' courses by publicising details of courses, and perhaps by arranging sponsorship or financial assistance for members wishing to attend a course. Courses vary, according to type and level. They may be residential, or span several evenings or weekends. Inevitably, costs are incurred by the trainee coach, which may be prohibitive.

Information
The governing bodies in sport often have books, booklets and leaflets available to aid coaches. If they do not produce their own publications, they may hold lists of relevant published material. Clubs should try to publicise information about these publications, and if possible keep a few books, leaflets or newsletters on the premises for use by members who coach.

One interesting way of teaching a skill is by use of film, which may be hired or bought, either from governing bodies or from commercial organisations. Films can be used during coaching sessions or as the focus for an instructional/social evening, which could be advertised in other clubs and sports centres, inviting a larger potential audience, and generating greater revenue from the bar.

The Sports Council publishes·a list, regularly updated, of sport-related books, as well as a catalogue of sports films and where to obtain them.

The National Coaching Foundation, formed in 1984, aims to provide opportunities for the development of knowledge and skills relevant to coaching, performance and participation at all levels. It is producing a selection of study units for coaches, covering topics such as safety and injury, sport and technology, and "mind over matter". The units are accompanied by video films and booklets.

Organisation
Coaching within a club can have a variety of aims. The club may wish to promote increased participation; to develop a junior section; to pro-duce a winning team.

6. COACHING, ACCIDENTS, INJURIES

Ideally, all coaching activities should be co-ordinated by a qualified coach, paid or unpaid. The club coach should participate in the selection and facilities committees. He or she should by supported by a team of volunteer coaches, who have preferably undertaken some training. Any coaching system, however informal, risks foundering if it depends on only one person, who may have to withdraw for illness or other reasons.

Apart from communicating with the players, team members or team captains, club coaches may be able to organise liaison with relevant specialists, who might include:

— national coach(es) for the sport;
— doctor;
— physiotherapist, or other relevant paramedical practitioner;
— physiologist;
— dietician;
— psychologist.

These experts may be used to advise on balanced training schedules. They may monitor, and if necessary amend, schedules for individuals or teams, guiding the coaches in safe conditioning and injury prevention methods.

Sessions

Coaching within a club may be a simple, informal session, where the coach spends time with the player(s), advising on obvious faults. Or the player may hire the services of the resident professional coach, for individual tuition. In either case, the coaching session will be more helpful if the coach has certain objectives in mind, and structures the session to fulfil these.

A club may choose to organise more ambitious coaching sessions, inviting senior or national coaches to conduct sessions lasting a full day or weekend. In order to increase the numbers participating, a few clubs may join together in this project. The sessions may be organised for specific groups, such as first teams, children, women or older participants.

When a club invites an outside coach to take a session, it should take note of the following points:

— the invitation should be made well in advance;
— the coach's fee, and subsidiary needs such as meals and travel expenses should be established, to make sure the club or participants can afford the costs;
— the number of likely participants should be ascertained in advance;
— the coach should be given an outline of what the club expects or requires of the session.

6. COACHING, ACCIDENTS, INJURIES

Once the coach has accepted the invitation, it is up to the club to organise the following:

1. The coach must receive clear directions on how to reach the club, or suitable travel arrangements must be organised.
2. Details of the session, including time, place and cost (if applicable) are circulated to all intending participants.
3. The location chosen should be suitable for the activity, and the numbers involved.
4. Any special requirements by the visiting coach, such as overhead projector, video equipment or training markings on the pitch or court, are provided.
5. If large numbers of participants are involved, club coaches and members should be willing to help the visiting coach. If this happens, time should be allowed before the session for a liaison meeting between the visiting coach and the volunteer helpers.
6. All the necessary equipment should be readily available, with spares of any items which might be broken or lost in the course of the session.
7. Refreshment breaks, for morning coffee, lunch, tea and/or supper, should be organised by extra helpers, so that as little time as possible is lost. If large numbers are involved, there should be several refreshment points, so that participants do not have to form one lengthy queue.
8. If possible, a secure area should be provided, where participants can safely leave their clothing and valuables. If this is not possible, players should be advised to keep valuable belongings where they can see them.
9. If the club's changing facilities are small, participants should be encouraged to change at home if possible, or, by arrangement, in other local clubs or sports centres. Alternatively, changing times can be "staggered", so that only small groups finish at one time.
10. Contingency plans should be made in case conditions disrupt the session: for instance, if the weather is wet the club should substitute indoor teaching sessions, or, if possible, arrange to use an all-weather or indoor playing surface in a nearby centre.
11. Indoor teaching sessions should not coincide with normal use of the club's facilities, such as the bar. If space is limited, the bar or lounge should be given exclusively to the coaching session, or another, exclusive, indoor conference room should be hired.
12. Club members not involved in the coaching session should be warned well in advance if use of facilities is to be disrupted.
13. Most coaching sessions end with a period of summing-up and questions. Time and space should be allowed for this.
14. The coach must be properly thanked, both in person at the end of

session, and in writing, possibly at the same time as the fee and expenses are paid. If any publicity is prompted by the session, copies of newspaper articles should be sent to the coach.

ACCIDENTS

Accidents may just happen, but they could be preventable. It is important for constant vigilance over safety factors and for continual improvement and updating of safety methods and systems to reduce risks for members, employees, visitors and the general public.

The house and ground committees are likely to be most directly involved with safety factors within the club. Some points to check are:

1. Fixed equipment should be secure.
2. Heavy loads and awkward items which have to be moved should be made as accessible and mobile as possible to minimise the risk of back injuries.
3. Maintenance and ground equipment, like tractors and mowers, should be kept safely. They should be inaccessible, if possible, with dangerous parts such as cutting blades properly covered when not in use.
4. Chemicals, fertilisers and other hazardous materials should be kept out of reach of children and vandals.
5. Ladders and scaffolding should be properly secured during maintenance work, and preferably made inaccessible to children and thieves when not in use.
6. Breakages, such as cracked windows and splintered wood, should be repaired immediately, and any hazardous debris removed completely.
7. Routine maintenance, like inspection of electrical wiring and plumbing systems, must be kept up regularly.
8. Storage areas should be kept clean and tidy, especially where potentially hazardous materials are involved such as the carbon dioxide cylinders in the bar.
9. Gangways, corridors and entrances should be kept clear, in case of fire. Over-crowding with furniture or machines in the communal areas of the clubhouse must be avoided.
10. Simple safety precautions, such as unplugging televisions and other electrical appliances from the mains, must be adhered to.

Fire precautions and procedures should be posted visibly around the club. Members need to know where the fire exits are; where the fire extinguishers are; where the nearest telephone is; and who to contact after a fire, in case evidence is needed for insurance or legal purposes.

First aid kits must be readily available, especially in areas of special risk, like the kitchen. Kits must be re-stocked regularly. Reporting accidents, however minor, should be encouraged. A book, with a pen attached, should be kept for this purpose, and staff and members made aware of it. Well-kept records would help to show if first-aid items are being misused. More seriously, if any litigation arose from an accident, an accurate immediate account of it could help simplify proceedings.

Clubs bear a great deal of the responsibility for making their premises safe, and this can be reflected in the choice of building and furnishing materials, as well as in the design and layout of the facilities. Clubs should also try to encourage members to take note of safety precautions. Suggestions for improving safety could be invited, perhaps with prizes on offer for the best suggestion. Modern films on safety can be entertaining as well as educational, and they can be used at social evenings, perhaps combined with coaching films, or even with popular entertainment.

If club members assume a corporate responsibility for safety factors, the avoidable accidents are less likely to happen.

INJURIES

Playing sport of any kind gives rise to the risk of injury. Recognising these risks, every club should be aware of and promote injury prevention. Accepting that not all injuries are avoidable, a club should provide some level of care and help for the injured sportsman.

Prevention
The risk of injury can be minimised if the club ensures that due regard is made to the following safety factors:

— playing conditions should be safe;
— the facility should be safe;
— equipment should be safe and safety equipment used;
— players should be encouraged to follow guidelines for safe body conditioning for their sport, with due regard for individual limitations and weaknesses;
— the rules of a game should be properly and fairly applied.

The people who can advise the club on aspects of safety in sport are trained groundstaff, engineers or maintenance staff responsible for the upkeep of the playing facilities or buildings, qualified coaches, medical and paramedical personnel, including doctors, physiotherapists, osteopaths, nurses, and qualified referees, judges, umpires or markers.

"It's OK Johnny, I've got a stretcher in my pack!"

Safe playing conditions. Weather conditions can seriously affect many sports. If a pitch is icy, frostbound or waterlogged, players may slip and fall, straining joints and muscles, or causing dangerous collisions with other players.

Wind and weather have a direct effect on the safety and enjoyment of such sports as hang gliding and sailing.

Very hot weather can cause dehydration in sportsmen whose fluid intake is not adequate, especially if they are involved in endurance sports like marathon running or cycling road races. Very cold conditions can lead to hypothermia, a special danger, again, for endurance sports.

Safe facilities. Play should not be allowed if a pitch, court or running track is not in a safe condition, for whatever reason. When new facilities are planned, safety factors must be included, even if these add to the capital and running costs.

Examples of safety factors in playing facilities are:

1. The floor of an indoor playing area should be clean and dry.
2. Play should never be allowed on a surface which is slippery, whether through grit, water leaked from the roof, condensation or incorrect polishing.
3. Rebound walls should not have any projections or jagged edges, and door handles should be properly recessed.

161

4. Lighting should be strong enough for good visibility, but not dazzling to the players.
5. Segmented mats, as for judo, should be securely joined, with no gaps or ridges.
6. Free standing basketball goals should be correctly weighted to prevent toppling.
7. Outdoor pitches should be correctly laid, so that sub-surface material, like glass or metal fragments, cannot rise to the surface.
8. Players should not be placed at risk from chemicals or fertilisers used over a playing surface.

Equipment safety. Players can help avoid injuries by maintaining their equipment properly, replacing worn or broken items. Worn equipment may pose a hazard to the player himself, or to other players, or both. Some sports have recognised special risks, and imposed safety measures, such as the introduction of speed restricting governors in motor sports.

Other considerations of equipment safety include:

— court shoes should not have worn, slippery soles, most sports require at least some grip or traction underfoot;
— field boots should not have sharpened studs;
— cracked squash rackets should not be used;
— jewellery or safety pins should not be worn in combat sports like judo or karate;
— the bobble on the bow of a rowing shell should be securely in place.

Many sports make use of safety gear for participants. Clubs should try to keep up-to-date with new developments in safety equipment, and inform their members. Safety goggles for squash are an example of a safety item recognised as necessary within the sport, but not yet widely adopted because of design flaws. Governing bodies often recommend safety gear; sometimes players adopt certain items through awareness of their own safety. The goalkeeper in the medal-winning Great Britain hockey team in the 1984 Olympics kitted himself out in American ice hockey protective clothing, and made some spectacular saves.

Standard safety items include:

— helmets for motor cyclists, boxers, cricket batsmen, and hard hats for horse riders;
— face masks for fencers, field sport goalkeepers;
— mouthguards for boxers, rugby players;
— goggles for skiers, swimmers;
— shoulder, elbow and knee pads for American footballers, skateboarders;

— groin boxes for cricketers;
— shin pads for footballers, hockey players.

Safe body conditioning. Many injuries are caused because players subject themselves to greater effort and strain than their bodies can cope with. A player may undertake an unreasonably heavy training programme just before the start of the season, after a holiday. A beginner may try too hard, or practise too intently, with no background in a sport. Sports involving repetitive patterns of movement, like running and rowing, carry a strong risk of overuse injuries.

In children, this risk is magnified by the fact that growing bones are particularly badly adapted for repetitive stress. Another risk for children is playing games with adult-sized implements, like rackets or javelins.

Stiffness can play a part in muscle strains and tears. Muscles become stiff through over-work, if the player has done too much in preceding days, or they can be affected by cold or fatigue. Incomplete recovery from a previous injury, with resultant muscle shortening, can lead to further strains.

Important injury prevention measures are a full warm-up and warm-down and a carefully graduated sporting programme. A warm-up should last about fifteen minutes, or longer if the weather is very cold. Essential elements in the warm-up are passive, slow muscle stretching; gentle bouncing movements to loosen joints; some "rapid-fire" exercises, like bursts of sprints, skips or jumps; and some exercises involving the movements which will take place in the particular sport, such as shadow swinging for racket games, or imaginary kicks for football. The warm-down can be a shorter version of this format, concentrating especially on the passive stretching exercises. A warm shower should be taken immediately after exercise.

A graduated sports programme means that a player should never make any sudden change or increase in a routine which is to be repeated on successive days. Ideally, fitness is maintained with a certain level of activity throughout the year, and then increased with a controlled build-up for the competition season. Realistically, most players suffer from aches and stiffness after the first game of the season, or the first hard training session. The safe way to recover is to spend one or two days simply stretching the muscles, and perhaps going for gentle swims (if the stiffness was not caused by swimming training). Hard sport should not be undertaken until all the stiffness is gone. If the player does participate despite residual stiffness, there is a strong risk of muscle strain.

After a lay-off, whether for injury, illness or other reasons, no player should be encouraged to resume sport at the same intensity as before the lay-off. A gradual re-start is essential.

If a player gets an injury, he should make a complete recovery before re-starting sport, if possible under specialist supervision. Trying out an injury before it is fully healed inevitably leads to further breakdown. Head injuries in particular require caution. Governing bodies of sports such as boxing and rugby have recognised that any head injury requires a medical check, followed by a period of "suspension" during which the injured player is not allowed to participate in sport.

The sportsman must also be aware of the importance of fatigue and illness in relation to sport. Although it is generally safe to play through a common cold, any virus, causing a raised temperature, carries a strong risk of heart damage if the sportsman chooses to ignore it. Excessive fatigue may be a symptom of illness. No sportsman should try to continue his activity if it is simply making him more tired. Any sportsman with doubts about his health, whether about illness, or in relation to continuing, resuming or starting a sport, would be well advised to check with his doctor first.

Diet is another important part of the sportsman's background. Foodstuffs provide essential energy and any sportsman's diet should be well-balanced, with regular meals. Fluid intake is vital in preventing cramp and dehydration, so every sportsman should be encouraged to take plenty of water and dilute drinks, complemented by moderate salt on his food. Timing of meals should allow the sportsman not to play on either a full or an empty stomach. He should allow four hours digestion time after a heavy meal, but can take light snacks two hours or less before doing his sport.

Clubs should be aware of their responsibility in promoting their players' health. In particular, no player should be forced or pressurised to turn out for a team if he is still suffering from an illness or injury. The team may or may not benefit from the player's presence, but the player himself will certainly suffer.

Applying the rules. Many sports contain obvious risks of collision and dangerous confrontation. In combat sports, the referee stops the bout when harm is threatened, and it is part of the discipline of these sports that the participant stops short of causing actual harm to a losing opponent. The knock-out is the most dangerous inherent part of these sports, which cannot be controlled by rules, and it is the main reason for the growing demand for boxers to use headguards, or for the sport of boxing to be banned.

In many team body-contact sports, such as rugby, the referee has to prevent foul or reckless play. Rules are often formulated to prevent dangerous play, for instance the "let" and "point" rules in squash. Size matching is also an important safety rule applied to contact and combat sports. Designed to prevent unbalanced confrontations and unfairness, it also leads to some problems: for instance, sportsmen may take extreme measures to "make the weight" in rowing, judo or karate, if they believe they have a better chance of winning in a lighter category than their own; and heavyweight amateur wrestling covers such a wide span that there is still a strong chance of unequal opponents being pitted against each other.

Specifically to protect children from events which might harm them, some governing bodies have introduced age limits. The International Amateur Athletics Federation gives 18 as the minimum age for entry to official marathon races, because the long distance carries a strong risk of disrupting bone growth during the teenage years.

Clubs should encourage members to take courses as referees, umpires, judges and markers, so that games within the club can be properly officiated. Some governing bodies will organise such courses within individual clubs, provided that a reasonable turnout can be ensured. If players can also be involved in the courses, they may learn respect for their potential referees, and sympathy for refereeing problems.

If no club members wish to become involved in officiating, the club should ensure that any competition is properly officiated by invited referees to ensure safe, fair play.

Treatment
Although this book is not designed to discuss first aid techniques and medical matters, two points may indicate how important it is for first aid to be carried out efficiently and swiftly, if a major accident happens in a sport:

1. If the brain is deprived of oxygen, it can normally survive for about four minutes before its cells die off, causing irreparable harm. When a person has been exercising hard, this survival time is reduced to only about eighteen seconds.
2. If a person with severe spinal injury is badly handled after his accident, permanent paralysis may occur.

Clubs should therefore encourage members to take first aid qualifications, and, if possible, keep a record of those who have. The more people who know what to do in an emergency, whether they are playing members, coaches or club staff, the better any casualty in the club will be treated.

First aid courses are organised by the St John's Ambulance Brigade (St Andrew's Ambulance Brigade in Scotland), and the British Red Cross Association. Courses are organised as evening classes, or, more intensively, over several days at a time. The cost of courses is very modest and details can be obtained from the organisations themselves (headquarters or regional offices) or from a local library.

Many clubs list among their members practitioners such as doctors, dentists, physiotherapists, chiropodists, osteopaths and nurses. Most of these will already be trained in first aid, and may be willing to teach other members, as well as helping in any emergency. Although these practitioners may be willing to give their time and expertise, the club must understand that they are governed by rules, such as the one preventing them from treating a patient without reference to the patient's general practitioner, and the rule prohibiting advertising. Members must take care not to abuse a practitioner's goodwill.

First aid kits can be bought made-up from a variety of pharmaceutical companies. Some are geared to cover accidents in the working environment, others sports injuries. Costs vary widely according to the type of kit. Portable kits may be needed if accidents happen outside the clubhouse. Larger items should be kept accessible within the club, notably stretchers and resuscitation outfits. Clean water and ice should be readily available for first aid purposes. If it is some distance from clubhouse to pitch, fresh water for cleansing wounds should be kept by the side of the pitch in a flask, with ice cubes or flakes in a cool box.

Useful items for inclusion in a portable first aid kit are:

— chemical ice packs;
— sticking plasters;
— stocking or tubular bandage (brand name: Tubigrip);
— butterfly plasters;
— sterile swabs (gauze);
— sterile dressings (brand name: Melolin, gauze with film backing);
— healing gel (brand names: Second Skin, Plastic Skin);
— cotton wool;
— scissors and safety pins;
— heparinoid cream (brand names: Hirudoid, Lasonil);
— sterile needles;
— inflatable splints;
— conforming bandages (open-weave, light cotton);
— crepe bandages;
— triangular bandages (slings).

Voluntary organisations like St John's Ambulance and the British Red Cross Association may provide trained personnel for matches and events. For large events a club must provide as much first-aid cover as possible, both for the participants and for the spectators. Organisations should be given as much notice as possible (about one month) with cover supplied depending on several factors:

1. Will cover be needed for players and/or crowd?
2. Are other agencies involved?

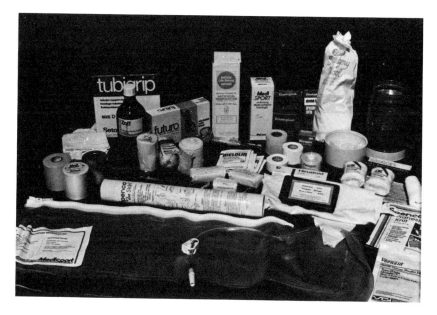

(Photograph by Vivian Grisogono)

Some useful items which ought to be included in any first-aid kit.

3. How many players and spectators are involved?
4. How long will cover be required?
5. What is the age and sex of those attending?
6. What facilities (treatment area, hot and cold water, telephone) are available?

Normally the voluntary organisations will provide the service without a set fee, although the club is expected to make a donation to the organisation's funds.

The club should also try to arrange for a doctor to be present on match days. He could be a member, paid in kind, or a local doctor attending for an agreed fee. In some sports, like boxing, the presence of a doctor is essential for official sanction of a match. In other sports, like rugby, it is highly advisable to have a doctor on hand, in case of major accidents.

If there are enough local enthusiasts, clubs may be able to set up their own injuries treatment unit for their members. Doctors, physiotherapists and perhaps chiropodists and osteopaths, may hold sessions in the club. They would need a room or larger area which could be curtained off, with couches and perhaps some electrotherapy equipment. Capital costs would have to be borne by the club, unless the practitioners hired the space, and set up the injuries unit as a private, fee-paying venture.

Whether or not a club has treatment facilities on the premises, it must publicise details of the nearest hospital casualty department, and travel details, if a casualty is to be transported by car, not using the ambulance service. Details of emergency dental services should also be posted; these can be obtained from the local community health service.

If the club does not provide its own treatment service for injuries, it should provide details of the nearest sports injury clinic. The ethical ban on advertising may prevent the club from posting these addresses on the noticeboard, but there is nothing to prevent a club from noting the details and making them available to members on request. Alternatively, members can contact local hospitals directly for information on sports clinics, or medical associations will provide information on local people treating sports injuries. Some regional sports councils keep a directory of clinics and practitioners in sports medicine.

In many cases, treatment for injuries is not obtainable under the National Health Service. Sportsmen needing treatment may have to obtain it in the private sector. Usually, the sportsman will be referred to a chartered physiotherapist, recognised by the initials MCSP following the name, or an osteopath, designated by the initials DO or MO. Medical insurance will often cover the cost of treatment from an ethical practitioner like a chartered physiotherapist, provided that the patient has gone to the physiotherapist via his general practitioner. British United Provident Association (BUPA), Private Patients' Plan (PPP) and Western Provident Association (WPA) will all cover physiotherapy fees, up to a certain limit, besides providing full cover against the cost of hospitalisation and surgery. MILAS Sportsplan, a special sports insurance, covers physiotherapy fees in part, as well as providing cover against loss of equipment, death and disability, and cash in case of hospitalisation.

Clubs can offer their members a vital service by informing them of the availability of medical and paramedical treatment, and insurance against sporting hazards.

Summary

Coaching, Accidents, Injuries

1. Coaching
Coaching is conducted mainly at two levels—recreational where skills are learnt and elite where the winning of competition is paramount.
At all levels there are four factors connected with coaching:
    technique;
    fitness training;
    tactics;
    enthusiasm.

2. Coaches' characteristics
Coaches must possess certain characteristics to teach a sport efficiently:
    communication;
    technical expertise;
    skill analysis;
    understanding of the sport;
    understanding of body mechanics.

3. Coaching qualifications
Qualified players and officials can give more back to the club.

4. Coaching information
Information from many sources allows coaches to function more efficiently.

5. Organised coaching
This section advises who the coach should liaise with and how to convey advice to club members in the most efficient way.

6. Accidents
How to recognise the most common causes of accidents and how to prevent them.

7. Injuries
Ways that injuries can be prevented and treated on the playing
field are discussed in full with specific examples. These are dealt
with under the headings:
>safe playing conditions;
>safe facilities;
>equipment safety;
>safe body conditioning;
>applying the rules.

---

8. Contents of a sports first aid kit
Items for inclusion in a portable first aid kit are listed. A great
improvement on the "magic sponge".

---

9. Help from medical practitioners
The role of doctors and paramedics and more importantly their
availability is discussed as is the location of sports injury clinics
and the services offered by medical insurance companies.

Appendix A
Case studies

Two entirely different voluntary sports groups who wish to develop their club's facilities are considered here. Although this is a theoretical exercise, the checklist of action taken will be of assistance to all clubs. The aim is to bring together points made throughout the book.

Example A: A group in a medium-size village which has a little light industry and a wide age distribution with an above average car ownership is given a five acre grass field, adjacent to a main road, to develop by a wealthy benefactor.

Example B: An empty derelict two-storey factory with basement, and adjacent yard, in an inner city area with typical problems —high unemployment, disproportionate senior citizens group, low income levels—is purchased for a nominal price by a local community group.

EXAMPLE A

The group must decide on how the club will administer the land and the activities to be carried out there. Once this has been done a development plan can be implemented.

To minimise the liability of members and to take advantage of financial inducements, such as covenants and mandatory rate relief, the group decides to form a charity. It can either do this by employing a solicitor who is experienced in charity formation or it can do the work itself. In the former case, the Law Society should be contacted. With the latter, the group should approach the Charity Commission to look at accepted Articles of Association and Memoranda of similar groups. The aims of the group will probably be satisfied by the wording in Chapter Two of this book. Further draft documents have been produced by the National Council for Voluntary Organisations (NCVO). The club should formulate a constitution and submit it to the Charity Commission for their approval. Possible items for insertion are detailed in Chapter One.

APPENDIX A

The club will need to function while this process is being carried out and the best action is to open a current bank account. Perhaps a fund raising evening to launch the club will produce some deposit money.

At a meeting, a committee should be elected to check the rules and the appropriate people should be approached to serve on it, e.g. builder, vicar, solicitor, teacher, local farmer. A chairman should be elected and a planning team co-opted to look at the options for the field.

Organisations such as the Sports Council, local authority and public services should be consulted and the sources of assistance, financial and practical, should be ascertained. Market research into the sporting and social needs of the local population should be organised. A mix of activities to appeal to the majority of people should be the objective.

A five acre site could cater for one football pitch, one hockey pitch, a cricket square, two floodlit tennis courts, a clubhouse with a small sports hall, children's play equipment, car parking, landscaping and necessary fencing. Estimates of costs should be gathered from experts such as the Sports Turf Research Institute for the grass playing area and an architect and building contractors for the clubhouse. Using their estimates and other information sources, such as the National Playing Fields Association cost guide, a budget figure should be determined. Maintenance costs must be borne in mind and the provision of an artificial surface, such as a cricket pitch, may prove advantageous in the long term although more expensive initially.

The club should divide its development into stages and invest its money in the activities which will bring quickest results in terms of interest and revenue. See Figure 3 at the end of this Appendix for ideas on the design of a clubhouse.

As building and layout costs vary across the country and within regions, and are affected by site considerations, it is difficult to generalise on this subject.

Depending on the reaction of the grant aiding bodies to the costings, the field could be developed as follows:

Phase 1
1. Drainage and preparation of the pitches and the formation of a cricket square.
2. Construction of a clubhouse with the following:
   — four changing rooms, two men's and two women's (plus showers);
   — officials' room;
   — hall big enough for recreational badminton;
   — bar/lounge;

— kitchen;
— storage space;
— smaller room for committee meetings, first aid, table tennis;
— connection to mains services—drainage, water, power.
Figure 2 shows how comparative circulation diagrams can be constructed to show the relationships between facilities for a small and a larger clubhouse for consideration by those concerned. Figure 3 shows how these diagrams may then be converted into plans for an actual building.

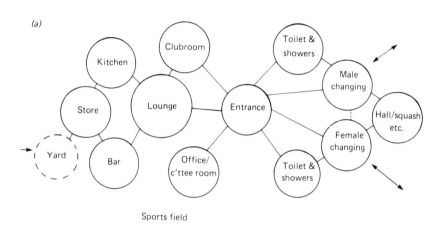

Fig. 2. Circulation diagrams for (a) a large, and (b) a smaller clubhouse.

3. Construction of hard play area big enough for two tennis courts with ducting for future floodlights.

APPENDIX A

Key

E: Equipment store   O: Officials changing
KS: Kitchen store   m: Male toilet
PR: Plant room   f: Female toilet
FC: Female changing   BS: Bar store
MC: Male changing

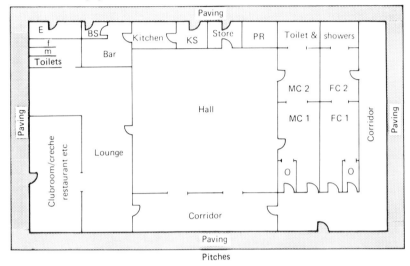

Fig. 3. Design for a clubhouse (not to scale). Note the following:

1. There is only one entrance which can lead players towards the changing rooms. This assists security.
2. Paving outside the clubhouse reduces the amount of mud and dirt being brought into the building and allows heavy items, e.g. barrels, to be stored.
3. The lounge/bar and clubroom overlook the playing area.
4. The bar, kitchen and lounge can service the hall while being separate from it.
5. The clubroom area can have a number of uses, especially if the partition walls are retractable, e.g. creche, meals area.
6. Outside doors into bar store, kitchen store and store should be double width to facilitate ease of entry.
7. Officials' and players' changing accommodation is separate.
8. The barrier wall between the corridor and the hall could be retractable. This would allow natural light to enter through outside windows when it is "open" and provide a barrier when privacy is needed. Artificial lights will not be needed all the time.
9. The door between the hall and the storage area should be recessed with safety handles (lockable).
10. Natural light will also enter the hall via the kitchen, as part of the kitchen should incorporate a service counter protected either by a grille or an "up and over" roller blind.
11. The doors leading onto the hall from the male changing rooms 1 and 2 can be secured at times to deter players entering the hall for whatever reasons. A notice about this can be affixed to the dressing room walls. It is necessary to ensure that safety regulations, especially those relating to fire, are observed.
12. Although toilets and washing facilities servicing the bar and changing rooms

174

are at opposite ends of the building, other functions such as the bar and kitchen will also need access to water and drainage systems. Although the distance is relatively long they are, however, logically arranged.

Phase 2
1. Completion of cricket square including one artificial pitch.
2. Use of pitches in second winter.
3. Siting of play equipment.

Phase 3
1. Construction of two squash courts.
2. Completion of children's playground.
3. Erection of hard play area floodlights.

Phase 4
Construction of a bowls green.

If the club carries out this scheme it can budget accordingly and provide cash flow projections when applying for aid.

Much of the building work of the clubhouse could be done by voluntary labour under skilled supervision, including:

— site clearance;
— provision of storage area;
— excavation and levelling;
— concreting and foundations;
— drainage:
— concreting of floors;
— insulation;
— paths;
— painting;
— fencing.

Expert advice both before and during the construction should be sought. If club members include plumbers, carpenters, electricians, roofers the cost of other parts of the work will be reduced and savings will be effected on VAT. Work on outside areas such as pitches can also be carried out by volunteer labour in many cases.

Sources of income could be:

— donations—individuals and firms;
— fund raising events;
— memberships, including life memberships;
— deferred loans;
— bank loans;
— Sports Council;
— governing body of sport;
— parish council grants;
— Manpower Services Commission input;
— National Playing Fields Association.

APPENDIX A

Once the project is completed it is important for it to be well programmed with the maximum use possible. Specific tasks to put the finishing touches are design for the sign at the entrance to the club's facilities; the contents of the rule book should be well thought out and, finally, the facilities should be kept under review with alternatives being introduced when necessary (e.g. weight equipment being sited in a squash court if demand falls off, introduction of indoor bowls in the hall instead of badminton).

It is important that everyone should be made welcome and feel able to contribute to the club.

EXAMPLE B

Although the factory should be in good structural repair, this will have to be checked by an architect and structural engineer. If the results are satisfactory, the group can decide on the activities to be organised. Discussions will have to be held with the local planning department about change of use and the rating department to ascertain financial implications.

The activities should appeal to as many groups as possible and if physical conditions allow the following could take place:

Basement   — boxing, shooting or weightlifting.
Ground floor — tennis, badminton, martial arts, general sport use.
First floor   — restaurant/bar, tennis, creche, aerobics, general use.
Yard   — all-weather kickabout area, bowls.

The primary need will be to generate income. The facilities to give quickest returns for least investment would be:

Basement   — weightlifting/weight-training (equipment leased).
Ground floor — badminton/tennis, changing rooms.
First floor   — restaurant/bar with aerobics, or dance area and viewing gallery over ground floor.
Yard   — all-weather bowls surface.

If shooting is incorporated, extra safety measures approved by the police and the army will be needed, as well as additional measures for prevention of noise and lead pollution.

On the ground floor the ceiling height will be the crucial factor, with alternative uses to badminton being introduced if necessary. The cost of lighting and spectator provision could be expensive, especially if additional exits have to be built.

On the first floor there should be maximum usable space to encourage as many different activities as possible. A good restaurant/bar will generate income and be complementary to the other facilities.

In the yard, an all-weather bowls area will allow play all year round and may be attractive to another under-provided group—the 45+.

In view of the likelihood of the facilities being popular and possibly overused, the club could be organised as a members' club formed as a company with personal liability limited by guarantee. By adopting this method membership applications can be restricted. (This would not be possible if the club was a charity.) As the facility is likely to be used throughout most of the day, the club should consider appointing a manager. The NCVO book *Employing Staff in Voluntary Organisations* should be consulted as a source of information.

Although there will be mains connections, alterations and refurbishments to the building will be necessary. Often the cost of refurbishing a building is greater than building anew as self-help is not likely to be so relevant.

There are a number of funding agencies who could be interested in this project. Applications should definitely be made to the following:

— Sports Council;
— Department of the Environment;
— metropolitan area;
— local authority (borough);
— commercial financial bodies.

Discussion should be held with these organisations from the outset.

Although these are only brief examples showing what is possible in a sports project carried out by voluntary organisations, they demonstrate the four headings, which recur throughout this book, needing attention to ensure success. These are:

— time;
— organisation;
— money;
— information.

Appendix B
Glossary of Financial Terms

accumulated reserve (general reserve/capital account) This represents the net worth of the organisation, i.e. the value of all the assets less the value of all liabilities.

balance sheet A statement which shows a summary of the balances in the accounts of the organisation. Traditionally assets are shown on the right hand, liabilities on the left. However, it is becoming more common for this information to be prepared in a vertical form. A supporting profit and loss account or income and expenditure record must also be seen.

brewery loan The loan is usually secured on club property (known as a "charge") and/or by personal guarantee, and is conditional although often interest free. The conditions could stipulate a "tied" or part tied trade with the brewery offering the loan. Repayment can be in cash or calculated on a regular barellage figure (calculated on each barrel of beer or equivalent sold; the loan decreases by a predetermined amount at different levels of sales).

capital expenditure Expenditure of a major nature—buildings, equipment, freehold.

cash flow projection A method whereby a club can forecast anticipated income and expenditure over a certain period. A cash flow projection is often requested by organisations who have been asked to provide financial assistance towards the cost of a club's project. Projections are normally most accurate over a short period (one to two years) and are based on records that the club may possess—accounts, membership records. They are a useful tool for comparing actual results with anticipated figures. If something is not as expected, investigations and necessary action should be carried out.

current assets These are club assets which are likely to be realisable within a maximum of one year. These include debtors (who owe the club money), certain investments and certain stocks. See also **liquid assets**.

current liabilities These are debts to other people, i.e. creditors, short-term loans,

178

overdrafts, subscriptions paid in advance which are likely to fall due for payment within one year. Loans will, however, have agreed repayment dates.

debentures A debenture is a form of loan. A club may raise funds by offering debentures to members. The loan is secured. In the event of the club dissolving, debenture holders stand in front of other loans for repayment.

debt Money or goods owed to someone else.

deferred loans In the course of a building scheme a club may borrow money to finance stage payments to contractors. If it does not wish to commence repayments on the borrowed money straight away a deferred loan could be negotiated. The loan repayment would then normally begin once the building is completed and earning money. Because of the delay in starting repayments, the rate of interest will probably be higher.

depreciation Depreciation is the mechanism for writing off the cost of an asset over what is deemed to be its useful life. The most common items depreciated are sports equipment, cars and maintenance equipment. Often a repairs or renewal fund will be built up out of profits for the replacement of worn out assets. Many replacement items will not be eligible for grant aid from bodies such as the Sports Council.

discounted cash flow (DCF) A tool for estimating how much needs to be invested today to generate a target amount in the future. Also compares the expected income from an investment and the value of the cash equivalent at today's prices (worth). Examples are contained in Chapter Four.

dividend This is a share of the profits of an incorporated company (Ltd) given to shareholders, usually distributed annually. Not applicable to members' clubs usually. Clubs may be asked to adhere to this principle if they are seeking aid from public bodies.

fixed assets This usually refers to assets of a more permanent nature—land, buildings, major equipment, long leases. These are not regarded as liquid or easily cashable.

freehold A description of a type of ownership of a club's tenure on its facilities. Loans may be taken out using a freehold as security.

inflation The cumulative effect of rising prices. Cumulative is the important word. An item costing £100 now, will in five years time, with inflation at 6 per cent, cost £134.

lease A contract allowing a lessee the right to use a facility in exchange for a rent or premium given to the lessor who is usually the freeholder or head lessee. Usually valid for a particular period, a lease can contain break clauses and be split into a head lease with one or more sub leases.

leaseholder One whose security on land or buildings is held by virtue of a lease.

leasing Essentially this is a form of obtaining equipment (usually) without making a deposit payment as with hire purchase or commercial loans. A lease agreement gives the use of the equipment to the hirer in exchange for rental or a fee. The rental is paid on a regular basis and for a fixed term only. At the end of that term the user usually has the option to buy the equipment for a peppercorn sum or take out another lease agreement on new equipment. The old equipment would then be repossessed by the leasing company. The rental often compares very favourably with loan repayments for the same item.

licence A licensee holds a licence granted by a licensor which authorises a particular usage or activity, i.e. use of playing field. Often renewable annually.

limited company A limited company is a "body corporate". It has a single identity in business and in law and is not a collection of individuals as in a partnership. The limited company, as its name implies, was designed to protect trading individuals by allowing them to operate with limited financial liability. The extent of the liability of a limited company is measured by its share capital. A company may be limited by guarantee and have no share capital. In this instance, in the event of financial problems the guarantors would be called upon to provide the guaranteed sums. That would be the limit of their liability.

liquid assets These are items which can be realised at very short notice and include cash, some investments, certain stocks.

mortgage A mortgage is a secured property loan given by a mortgagee to a mortgagor. It is always a secured loan.

profit and loss account (income and expenditure a/c) This account is used to calculate the net profit or loss earned in a specified period. This document should be used in conjunction with the balance sheet if one is available. The account shows the operating costs of the club set against its revenue income. Some aspects, like the bar, are often separated within the account and a gross profit figure is then calculated. This is carried down as an item of income if a profit is made, or a loss if a deficit. Also shown are a number of very useful costs, e.g. staff costs, loan repayments (including overdrafts), insurance premiums paid, maintenance costs, domestic running expenses such as rates etc. The differences between profit and loss and income and expenditure accounts are not particularly important. Small voluntary clubs will tend to produce the former, while larger clubs will probably produce the latter.

receipts and payments accounts Less formalised form of accounting. A summary of all income received and cash payments made in the period.

revenue expenditure Expenditure that is of a recurring nature, e.g. rates, electricity. No organisation should *need* to borrow money to meet its revenue needs.

share capital (ordinary, preferential, cumulative) The value of all the shares issued by a limited company. A preference share has priority over an ordinary share when limited profits are being disbursed. Cumulative dividends are added if not enough profit is made in any year.

stock-in-hand Usable stock of a bar or kitchen with which

the next period's trading will commence, i.e. next day, month or year.

trading account A simple account designed to show the net profit or loss on the operation of only one activity. Most commonly used for the bar or kitchen.

value added tax (VAT) An indirect tax which is charged on goods and services in the course of furtherance of a business. A club with taxable supplies (subs, joining fees, sale of goods, letting fees) in excess of (currently) £19,500 p.a. is required to register with Customs and Excise. The current rate of VAT is 15 per cent. Officials should liaise closely with and make use of the publications of the Customs and Excise.

working capital The working capital balance is obtained by deducting current liabilities from current assets.

Appendix C

A Specimen Income and Expenditure Account and Balance Sheet

INCOME AND EXPENDITURE ACCOUNT YEAR ENDED 31 MARCH 1985

Anywhere Sports and Social Club

Expenditure	1985 £	1984 £
Rates	264	221
Water, light and heating	308	268
Cleaning	103	243
Building maintenance	631	472
Insurances	265	239
Telephone	18	80
Postage and printing	39	57
Bar sundries	20	20
Upkeep of pitches	9	902
Disposable equipment, e.g. balls	249	568
Tournament expenses	43	59
Affiliation fees	118	55
Mortgage interest (gross)	53	63
Sundry expenses	—	4
Depreciation: clubhouse	178	179
furniture and equipment	135	128
Excess of income over expenditure	1,177	
	3,610	3,558
Balance transferred to Capital Account	177	
Transfer to Pitch Reserve Account	1,000	
	£1,177	

Income	1985 £	1984 £
Bar gross profit:		
Sales: Less VAT	7,935	8,556
Less: purchases, adjusted for stocks	6,318	7,222
	1,617	1,334
Subscriptions:		
Playing	1,210	830
Social	216	254
"100 club" receipts less prizes	252	289
Deposit interest	82	59
Wayleaves	6	6
Entertainments	70	9
Machine profit	157	
Excess of expenditure over income	—	777
	3,610	3,558
Balance brought down	1,177	
	£1,177	

BALANCE SHEET YEAR ENDED 31 MARCH 1985

Anywhere Sports and Social Club

	£	1985 £	1984 £
Capital Account			
At 1 April 1984	3,245		
Add: Profit for year	177		
		3,422	3,245
Reserve for Pitches			
At 1 April 1984	1,000		
Transfer from I&E a/c	—		
Less: Expenditure	—		
		1,000	715
Mortgage on Freehold Land			
Advanced in 1970	2,500		
Less: Repaid to date	1,772		
		728	895
Creditors		357	715
		5,507	4,855

	£	1985 £	1984 £
Fixed Assets			
Freehold land			
At cost	2,570		
Less: Sales proceeds in 1980	300		
		2,270	2,270
Pavilion			
At cost	3,578		
Less: Depreciation to date	3,041		
		537	715
Furniture, fittings and equipment			
At cost	1,809		
Less: Depreciation to date	1,592		
		217	202
		3,024	3,187
Current Assets			
Cash at bank and at hand	1,406		828
Building society deposit	11		10
Premium bonds	100		100
Debtors and prepayments	297		224
Bar stock	669		506
		2,483	
		5,507	4,855

A. Honest-Man
Hon. Treasurer

Report of the Auditors to the Members of Anywhere Sports and Social Club
We certify that we have examined the books and vouchers of the Club and that in our opinion the above Balance Sheet and Income and Expenditure Account are in accordance therewith and show a true and fair view of the state of the affairs of the Club.

Cal Culator
A. B. A. Cus
Hon. Auditors

1 June 1985

Appendix D
Suggested Layout for a
Fund-raising Brochure for a
New Facility

COVER

1. The name of the club (whether new or existing).
2. An illustration or photograph of the sport the project will help, or an impression or photograph of a model of the building (if one is to be built).

PAGE ONE

The need for the new project should be briefly set out. This will include a description of the locality which will be served (with population size) and mention of any official reports which have been published stating any deficiency which the project is expected to remedy. Results of any surveys indicating public support can be stated. A map could be drawn showing the distance inhabitants in the locality have to travel to reach comparable facilities.

If a particular sport is to be catered for, its advantages should be stated, e.g. cheapness, attraction to many groups, little equipment needed.

PAGE TWO

The site
A brief description of the site for the new facility should be complemented by a clear site plan with neighbouring roads and well-known landmarks, e.g. public houses, churches, hospitals, well marked. Public transport features, such as bus stops and railway stations, will assist those people who do not own a private vehicle. Car parking space and possible future expansion plans should be indicated.

APPENDIX D.

The club

The planned facilities within the club, e.g. number of pitches, flood-lighting, children's areas, courts, changing and social facilities should be listed with proposed activities like internal leagues and affiliation to outside bodies described. This will stimulate interest.

The level(s) of potential members to be encouraged should be as wide as possible. If advice has been sought from outside experts, e.g. the governing body of the sport, local authority and Arts or Sports Council, this will indicate that the project has been properly thought through.

A detailed outline plan would be useful to help people understand what the project will look like.

PAGE THREE

Financing the project

The *capital* cost should be stated with details of any money which has been promised, e.g. by the local authority by means of grant or loan. Other bodies who have expressed an interest should be listed. The reader's attention should be brought to the categories of assistance available, e.g. individual loans, donations, standing orders, covenants (if a charity), corporate donations/loans.

The *running* costs should be stated with an estimate of how these could be financed.

These details could then be shown in tabular form as follows:

Capital costs	£
Playing facilities, e.g. pitches, courts	100,000
Changing and other facilities	25,000
	125,000

Fundraising	
Local authority assistance	40,000
Bank loan	35,000
Other grants and loans	10,000
Corporate membership and sponsorship	10,000
Private fundraising	20,000
Brewery input	10,000
	125,000

Annual running costs	
Income	
Membership fees (250 members)	7,500
Other receipts, e.g. bar, catering machines	15,000
	22,500

APPENDIX D

Expenditure

Running building, pitches	6,000	
Staffing, cleaning	4,000	
Contingencies	2,000	
	———	12,000

Therefore balance available for interest
and capital repayments   10,500

PAGE FOUR

Management style

A clear statement should be made about the management style of the facility and/or club. Emphasis should be laid on the fact that the club is voluntary and not profit distributing.

The committee structure should be set out and all represented groups should be mentioned. If there is a current committee or planning group responsible for the project it should be mentioned. A contact address and telephone number would be useful.

Application form

An application form (easy tear off variety) should carry details about membership fees and other forms of assistance which could be given to make the project a success.

GENERAL POINTS

Although they help make the brochure more eyecatching and attractive, photographs, and especially colour reproduction, will dramatically increase costs.

The cover is most important in attracting attention and a graphic artist whether employed by the club or associated with the club should be commissioned to design it. The brochure must be clearly printed with bold type. It should not be too big with pages not exceeding 14 cm × 30 cm. It should have two folds at most.

It is most important for detailed thought to be given to the layout and content of the appeals brochure as this could determine the success, or otherwise, of the fundraising effort. It must also attract the "locals", the potential customers of the new facility.

Appendix E
Useful Addresses

SPORTS ORGANISATIONS

British Association of National
  Coaches
Oak Lodge
Theobalds Park Road
Enfield
Middlesex
01-363 1506

British Association of Sports for
  the Disabled
Haywards House
Harvey Road
Aylesbury
Buckinghamshire
0296 27889

British Olympic Association
1 Church Row
Wandsworth Plain
London SW18 1EH
01-874 4764

Central Council for Physical
  Recreation
Francis House
Francis Street
London SW1P 1DE
01-828 3163

Football Association
16 Lancaster Gate
London W2 3LW
01-262 4542

Football Trust
PO Box 116
London SW19 3RD
01-388 4504

Institute of Groundsmanship
The Pavilion
Woughton-on-the-Green
Milton Keynes MK6 3EA
0908 663600

Institute of Leisure and Amenity
  Management
Ilam House
Lower Basildon
Reading RG8 9NE
0491 87 3558

Lawn Tennis Association
Barons Court
West Kensington
London W14 9EG
01-385 2366

National Coaching Foundation
4 College Close
Beckett Park
Leeds LS6 3QH
0532 744802

National Documentation Centre
for Sport PE and Recreation
PO Box 363
University of Birmingham
Birmingham B15 3TT
021-472 1301 ext. 2312

National Cricket Association
Lords Cricket Ground
London NW8 8QN
01-289 1611

The National Playing Fields
Association
25 Ovington Square
London SW3 1LQ
01-584 6445

Rugby Football Union
Whitton Road
Twickenham TW2 7RQ
01-892 8161

Sports Aid Foundation
16 Upper Woburn Place
London WC1
01-387 9380

Sports Council
(See **Government Agencies**)

Sports Turf Research Institute
Bingley
West Yorkshire BD16 1AX
0274 565131

Squash Rackets Association
Francis House
Francis Street
London SW1
01-828 3064

GOVERNMENT DEPARTMENTS

Department of Employment
Caxton House
Tothill Street
London SW1 9NA
01-213 3000

For EEC Social Fund enquiries:
Department of Employment
Overseas Division OB2
address as above
01-213 7623

Department of the Environment
PPMNT 1 Division
2 Marsham Street
London SW1P 3EB
01-212 3515

Department of the Environment
Urban Conservation and Historic
Buildings Division
Fortress House
25 Saville Row
London W1X 2BT
01-734 6010

Department of Health and Social
Security
Alexander Fleming House
London SE1 6BY
01-407 5522

Department of Transport
Regional offices of the Traffic
Commissioners
(*See telephone directories for
details*)

Home Office
Voluntary Services Unit
50 Queen Anne's Gate
London SW1H 9AT
01-213 7079

Inland Revenue
Somerset House
New Wing
Strand
London WC2R 1LB
01-438 6622

GOVERNMENT AGENCIES

Advisory, Conciliation and
  Arbitration Services (ACAS)
11–12 St James Square
London SW1Y 4LA
01-214 6000

Arts Council of Great Britain
  Information and Research
105 Piccadilly
London W1V 0AU
01-629 9495

Central Register for Charities
St Albans House
57–60 The Haymarket
London SW1Y 4QX
01-214 6000

Charity Commission
14 Ryder Street
St James's
London SW1Y 6AH
01-214 6000

Charity Commission
Graeme House
Derby Square
Liverpool L2 7SB
051-227 3191

Commission for New Towns
Glen House
Stag Place
London SW1E 5AJ
01-828 7722

Commission for Racial Equality
Elliott House
10–12 Allington Street
London SW1E 5EH
01-828 6022

Community Industries Ltd
24 Highbury Crescent
London N5 1RX
01-226 6663

Countryside Commission for
  England and Wales
John Dower House
Crescent Place
Cheltenham
Glos GL50 3RA
0242 521381

8 New Bond Street
Newtown
Powys SY16 2LU
0686 26799

and regional offices in
  Birmingham, Bristol,
  Cambridge, Leeds, London,
  Manchester, Newcastle-on-
  Tyne

Countryside Commission for
  Scotland
Battleby
Redgorton
Perth PH1 3EW
0738 27921

The Crafts Council
12 Waterloo Place
London SW1Y 4AU
01-930 4811

HM Customs and Excise
Kings Beam House
Mark Lane
London EO3R 7HE
01-283 8911

The Development Commission
11 Cowley Street
London SW1P 3NA
01-222 9134

Equal Opportunities Commission
Voluntary Organisations Unit
Overseas House
Quay Street
Manchester M3 3HN
061-833 9244

Chief Registrar for Friendly
  Societies
Registry of Friendly Societies
15 Great Marlborough Street
London W1Y 2AP
01-437 9992

English Tourist Board
4 Grosvenor Gardens
London SW1W 0DU
01-730 3400

and regional offices in
  Abingdon, Bolton, Eastleigh,
  Exeter, Ipswich, Lincoln,
  Newcastle-upon-Tyne,
  Tunbridge Wells, Windermere,
  Worcester, York

Health and Safety Executive
Baynards House
1 Chepstow Place
London W2 4TF
01-229 3456

For entertainments and sports
  grounds enforcement office:
Victoria House
Ormskirk Road
Preston PR1 1HH
0772 59321

(Also contact e.&s.g. officer at
  Health & Safety Exec. area
  offices)

Inland Revenue
Claims Branch
Magdalen House
Trinity Road
Bootle
Merseyside L69 9BB
051-922 6363

Manpower Services Commission
Corporate Services Division
Moorfoot
Sheffield, S. Yorks
0742 753275

Manpower Services Commission
Information Department
Selkirk House
High Holborn
London WC1
01-836 1213

For further details of Youth
  Training Scheme contact area
  board see telephone directory.
  For further details of Community Programme contact
  local Community Programme
  Link Team (from Job Centre).

Nature Conservancy Council
70 Castlegate
Grantham
Lincs NE31 6SH

Northern Ireland Tourist Board
River House
48 The High Street
Belfast
0232 31221

Office of Wages Councils
Steel House
11 Tothill Street
London SW1H 9NF
01-405 8454

APPENDIX E

Scottish Tourist Board
23 Ravelston Terrace
Edinburgh EH4 3EU
031-332 2433

Sports Council
16 Upper Woburn Place
London WC1H 0QP
01-388 1277

Sports Council Regional Offices:

Northern
County Court Building
Hallgarth Street
Durham DH1 3PB
0385 49595

North West
Byrom House
Quay Street
Manchester M3 5JF
061-834 0338

Yorkshire and Humberside
Coronet House
Queen Street
Leeds LS1 4PW
0532 436443

East Midland
26 Munsters Road
West Bridgford
Nottingham NG2 7PL
0602 821887

West Midlands
Metropolitan House
1 Hagley Road
Five Ways
Birmingham B16 8TT
021-454 3808

Eastern
26–28 Bromham Road
Bedford MK40 2QD
0234 44281

Greater London and South East
PO Box 480
Crystal Palace National Sports
  Centre
London SE19 2QB
01-778 8600

Southern
Watlington House
Watlington Street
Reading RG1 4RJ
0734 595616

South Western
Ashlands House
Ashlands
Crewkerne
Somerset TA18 7LQ
0460 73491

Sports Council for Scotland
1 St Colme Street
Edinburgh EH3 6AA
031-225 8411

Sports Council for Wales
National Sports Centre for Wales
Sophia Gardens
Cardiff CF1 9SW
0222 397571

Sports Council for Northern
  Ireland
2a Upper Malone Road
Belfast BT9 5LA
0232 661222

Welsh Tourist Board
Welcome House
Llandaff
Cardiff CF5 2YZ
0222 567701

LOCAL GOVERNMENT ORGANISATIONS

The Association of County
  Councils
66a Eaton Square
London SW1W 9BH
01-235 1200

The Association of District
  Councils
9 Buckingham Gate
London SW1E 6LE
01-828 7931

The Association of Metropolitan
  Authorities
36 Old Queen Street
London SW1H 9JE
01-222 8100

The London Boroughs
  Association
PO Box 240
Westminster City Hall
Victoria Street
London SW1E 6LE
01-828 8070

The National Association of
  Local Councils
108 Great Russell Street
London WC1B 3LD
01-637 1865

ASSOCIATIONS AND INSTITUTIONS

Association of British Sponsors
  of the Arts
Church Yard
Bath
Avon

Association of British Travel
  Agents
55 Newman Street
London W1
01-637 2444

British Insurance Brokers
  Association
10 Bevis Marks
London EC3
01-623 9043

Chartered Institution of
  Building Services
Delta House
222 Balham High Road
London SW12 9BS
01-675 5211

Royal Institute of British
  Architects
66 Portland Place
London W1
01-580 5533
01-323 0687 (clients' advisory
  service)

Royal Town Planning Institute
26 Portland Place
London W1N 4BE
01-636 9107

CHARITABLE ORGANISATIONS

Charities Aid Foundation
48 Pembury Road
Tonbridge
Kent TN9 2ID
0732 02323

Industrial Common Ownership
  Movement
The Corn Exchange
Leeds LS1 7BP
0532 461737

Kidsline
Online Leisure Information
  Company Ltd
44 Earlham Street
London WC2H 9LA
01-222 4640
01-222 8070 (information line)

Lords Taverners
1 Chester Street
London SW1X 7JD
01-245 6466

National Council for Voluntary
  Organisations
26 Bedford Square
London WC1
01-636 4066

National Federation of
  Community Organisations
8/9 Upper Street
London N1 0PQ
01-226 0189

MEDICAL AND RELATED
ORGANISATIONS

Association of Chartered
  Physiotherapists in Sports
  Medicine
The Secretary
Half Moon Place
Burwash Road
Heathfield
East Sussex
04352 4607

British Association of Sport
  and Medicine
The Secretary
Half Moon Place
Burwash Road
Heathfield
East Sussex
04352 4607

British Red Cross Association
9 Grosvenor Crescent
London SW1X 7EJ
01-235 5454

British School of Osteopathy
1 Suffolk Street
London SW1
01-930 9254

British United Provident
  Association
Provident House
Essex Street
London WC2
01-353 9451

Chartered Society of
  Physiotherapy
14 Bedford Row
London WC1
01-242 1941

MILAS Sportsplan Protection
  Insurance
45 Queens Square
Corby
Northamptonshire NN17 1PD
0536 201661

Private Patients Plan
Eynsham House
Tunbridge Wells
Kent TN1 2PL
0892 40111

St John Ambulance Brigade
1 Grosvenor Crescent
London SW1
01-235 5231

Western Provident Association
Culver House
Bristol BS1 5JE
0272 23495

APPENDIX E

REGULATORY BODIES

British Amusement and
  Catering Trades Association
122 Clapham Common
North Side
London SW4 9SB
01-228 4107

British Standards Institution
2 Park Street
London W1
01-629 9000

Companies Registration Office
Crown Way
Maindy
Cardiff CF4 3UZ

Gaming Board for Great Britain
Berkshire House
High Holborn
London WC1
01-240 0821

Gaming Board (for Lotteries)
Africa House
Kingsway
London WC2
01-404 5786

The Law Society
113 Chancery Lane
London WC2
01-242 1222

Lotteries Council
13 Dover Street
London W1X 3PA

Performing Rights Society Ltd
29/33 Berners Street
London W1P 4AA
01-580 5544

Phonographic Performance
Ltd
14 Ganton Street
London W1
01-437 0311

COMMERCIAL ORGANISATIONS

Automobile Association
Fanum House
New Coventry Street
London WC2
01-891 1400

British Gas Corporation
152 Grosvenor Road
London SW1
01-821 1444

British Rate and Data (BRAD)
76 Oxford Street
London W1
01-434 2233

Drugasar Ltd
Deans Road
Swinton
Manchester
061-793 8700

Electricity Council
30 Millbank
London SW1
01-834 2333

En Tout Cas
Syston
Leicester LE7 8NP
0533 696471

Royal Automobile Club
PO Box 100
RAC House
Lansdowne Road
Croydon
Surrey

Appendix F
Further Reading

Although this reading list refers to specific chapters some of the references will be applicable to more than one chapter. The following abbreviations will be used:

DE: Department of Employment
DHSS: Department of Health and Social Security
DoT: Department of Transport
NCVO: National Council for Voluntary Organisations (publications produced by the Bedford Square Press)
NPFA: National Playing Fields Association

Copies of Acts and Statutory Instruments are available from Her Majesty's Stationery Offices throughout the country.

CHAPTER ONE: MANAGEMENT OF A CLUB

Legislation
Charities Act, 1960
Defective Premises Act, 1972
Friendly Societies Act, 1974
Industrial and Provident Societies Acts, 1965 and 1968
Recreational Charities Act, 1958
Trustees Act, 1925

Books and booklets
M. Dockray, *Charity Trustees Guide* (NCVO) 1983
J. Edgington & S. Bates, *Legal Structures for Voluntary Organisations* (NCVO) 1984
En Tout Cas, *Handbook of Sports Club Management* (PA Management Consultants Ltd) 1981
C. P. Hill, *A guide for charity trustees* (Faber and Faber)
Michael Norton, *Investment of Charity Funds* (Directory of Social Change and the Charities Aid Foundation) 1985
M. A. Peters, *The Club Treasurer's Handbook* (Rose/Jordon Ltd) 1980

A. Phillips, *Charitable status: a practical handbook* (Inter-Action Imprint) 1980
Ian Shearman, *Shackleton on the Law and Practice of Meetings*, 7th ed. (Sweet and Maxwell) 1983
A. Tomlinson, *Leisure and the role of voluntary groups* (Sports Council) 1979
G. Torkildsen, *Leisure and Recreation Management* (E&F Spon) 1984

Leaflets and pamphlets
Companies Registration Office, *Incorporation of new companies— notes for guidance*
—, *Notes for the guidance of registered companies*
Industrial Common Ownership Movement, *Model for company limited by guarantee*
Liverpool City Council, Community Liaison Section, *How to compile, adopt and use a constitution: guidance notes for community associations*
National Confederation of Community Organisations, *Model constitution for community associations*
NCVO, *Legal responsibilities of members of committees of unincorporated voluntary organisations*, 1981
—, *Specimen constitution for an unincorporated voluntary organisation*, 1983
—, *Specimen deed for a charitable trust*, 1983
—, *Specimen Memorandum and Articles of Association for a company limited by guarantee*, 1983
Registrar of Friendly Societies, *Guide to the law relating to Friendly Societies and industrial assurance*

CHAPTER TWO: FINANCIAL ASPECTS OF A CLUB

Legislation
Betting and Gaming Duties Acts, 1972 and 1981
Gaming Act, 1968
Licensing Act, 1964 and Licensing (Occasional Permissions) Act, 1983
Local Government Act, 1972
Lotteries and Amusements Act, 1976
Wages Council Act, 1959

Books and booklets
R. Baldwin, *Taxation and Sport* (Arthur Anderson & Co.) 1985
H. Blume, *Fund raising: A comprehensive handbook* (Routledge and Kegan Paul) 1977
Cromer's Reference Book for the Employer (Cromer) annual
Cromer's Reference Book for the Smaller Business (Cromer) annual

D. Evans. *Supervisory Management* (Holt Business Texts) 1981
J. N. Martin, *Paterson's Licensing Acts*, 93rd ed. (Butterworth) 1985
NCVO, *Lotteries and gaming, voluntary organisations and the law* 1983
S. Townley and E. Grayson, *Sponsorship of Sports, Art and Leisure* (Sweet and Maxwell) 1984
G. Whitehead, *Bookkeeping Made Simple* (Heinemann) 1982

Leaflets and pamphlets
Customs and Excise, *VAT leaflet (701/34/04): VAT and competitions*
—, *VAT leaflet (701/5/84): Clubs and Associations*
Department of Employment, *Written statement of main terms and conditions of employment* (PL700)
Department of Health and Social Security, *Employer's guide to national insurance contributions* (NP15)
—, *National insurance and contract of service* (NI39)
—, *Class 1 contribution rates* (NP28)
—, *National insurance contribution rates* (NI208)
—, *National insurance guide for employers* (NI140)
Department of Transport, *Guide to the licensing of public service vehicles*
—, *A guide to public service vehicle operating licensing* (interim edition) PSV 437
Inland Revenue, *Employer's guide to PAYE* (P7)
—, *Income tax: Pay as you earn* (IR34)
Office of Wages Council, *Office of Wages Council Order LNR 159 (bar staff)*
—, *Office of Wages Council Order LNR 160 (stewards)*

CHAPTER THREE: FUNDING LARGE PROJECTS

Legislation
General Rate Act, 1967
Greater London Council General Powers Act, 1970
Local Government (Miscellaneous Provisions) Act, 1976
Physical Training and Recreation Acts, 1937 and 1958

Books and booklets
S. Bates, *Fundraising and grant aid for voluntary organisations—a guide to the literature available* (NCVO) 1981
H. Blume and M. Norton, *Raising money from government* (Directory of Social Change) 1977
Central Council for Physical Recreation, *You and the press; a guide for press officers at club and county level* 1983
Charities Aid Foundation, *The directory of grant making trusts* 1984

A. Darnborough and D. Kinrade, *Fundraising and grant aid* (Woodhead-Faulkner) 1980
A. Davison, *Grants from Europe* (NCVO) 1984
H. Griffiths, *Fundraising for Sport* (The Sports Council) 1985
NCVO, *Government grants: A guide for voluntary organisations* 1984

Leaflets and pamphlets

Customs and Excise, *VAT: Charities and other bodies engaged in new building projects on a self help basis* 1981
Department of Employment, *Young Workers Scheme* 1984
—, *Job Splitting Scheme* 1983
Manpower Services Commission, *Community Programme* 1983
—, *Voluntary Projects Programme* 1983
—, *Youth Training Scheme* 1983
National Playing Fields Association, *Financial policy for loan or grant aid* undated
The Sports Council, *Finance for sports facilities: how to get grants and loans for voluntary organisations* revised 1984
—, *Finance for sports facilities: grants for statutory bodies and commercial organisations* revised 1984
—, *Regional Participation Grants* revised 1983

CHAPTER FOUR: SPORTS CLUB FACILITIES

Legislation

Chronically Sick and Disabled Persons Act, 1970
Control of Pollution Act, 1972
Fire Prevention Act, 1971
Safety of Sports Grounds Act, 1975
Town and Country Planning Act, 1972

Books and booklets

British Standards Institution, *BS 5696 Playground Equipment*
D. A. Brodie and J. J. Thornhill, *Microcomputing in sport and PE* (Lepus Books) 1983
Ideal Home Magazine, *Book of Kitchens* revised 1984
NCVO, *The village hall: plan, design and build* 1983
—, *The village hall: managing your hall* 1979
—, *The village hall: maintenance* 1979
—, *The village hall: keeping accounts* 1980
NPFA, *Building Cost Guide* revised 1984
—, *Pitch and pavilion orientation design* 1979
—, *Playground management for local authorities* 1983
The Royal Town Planning Institute, *Where to find planning advice—a list of consultant firms* 1983

The Sports Council, *The handbook of sports and recreational building design* (4 volumes) (The Architectural Press) 1981

The Sports Council, *Specifications for Artificial Sports Surfaces* (3 volumes) 1985

Richard A. Sprenger, *Hygiene for Management* (Highfield Publications (Rotherham) Ltd) 1982

Pamphlets and articles

P. Hayes, "Natural turf versus synthetic surfaces: how the costs compare for Britain's football pitches," *Turf Management* March 1983

Lawn Tennis Association, *Tennis court surfaces* 1980

NPFA, Publications list, revised 1984

R. Narroway, "Computing: more than a sideline activity," *Sports Industry* Sept/Oct 1981

National Cricket Association, *"On the Mat": the non turf cricket pitch scene* undated

A. K. Nichols, "The use of microcomputers in recreation management," *Institute of Leisure and Amenity Management Journal* Vol. 2 No. 3, March 1984

Royal Institute of British Architects, *Thinking of building* 1976

—, *Use an architect*

Royal Town Planning Institute, *Can I object?* no date

—, *Should I appeal?* no date

—, *Your planning application* no date

T. Sedgwick, "Equipping for leisure," *Sports Industry* Mar/Apr 1982

The Sports Council, "A survey into the use and application of electric machines in sports clubs," *Sport and Leisure magazine* Nov/Dec 1984

CHAPTER FIVE: SPORTS CLUBS AND THE LAW

Legislation

The Copyright Act, 1956

Employer's Liability Compulsory Insurance Act, 1969

Equal Pay Act, 1970

Food and Drugs Act, 1955

Food and Drugs (Control of Premises) Act, 1976

Food and Drugs (Amendment) Act, 1982

Food Hygiene (General) Regulations, 1970

Health and Safety at Work etc Act, 1974

Employer's Health and Safety Policy Statement (Exceptions) Regulations, 1975

Race Relations Act, 1976

Sex Discrimination Act, 1975

Unfair Contract Terms Act, 1977

Books and booklets
E. Anthony and C. J. Acred, *A Guide to Licensing Law* 3rd ed. (Anthony & Berryman) 1980
Valerie Collins, *Recreation and the Law* (E&FN Spon) 1985
D. G. Cracknell, *Law relating to charities*, 2nd ed. (Oyez Longman) 1983
The Diagram Group, *Sports Laws* (J. M. Dent and Sons Ltd) 1983
David Field, *Practical Club Law* (Sweet and Maxwell) 1979
F. Gladstone, *Charity law and social justice* (NCVO) 1982
E. Grayson, *Sport and the law* (Daily Telegraph Publications)
Health and Safety Executive, *Guidance notes on employers' policy statement for Health and Safety at Work* revised 1984
J. F. Josling and L. Alexander, *The law of clubs* (Oyez Longman) 5th ed. 1984
S. Kurowska, *Employing people in voluntary organisations* (NCVO) 1984
The Law Society, *The Solicitor's Regional Directory* 1985
—, *The Solicitor's and Barrister's Directory and Diary* 1985
Performing Rights Society, *Yearbook* annual

Pamphlets and articles
National Federation of Community Organisations, *Bars, charities and the law*
Performing Rights Society, *Music, the Law and You!* 1983

CHAPTER SIX: COACHING, ACCIDENTS, INJURIES

Books and booklets
British Red Cross Association, *Services in hospitals and the community* annual
First Aid Manual—Emergency procedures for everyone at home, at work or at leisure (Dorling Kindersley) 1982. Approved by the Red Cross, St John and St Andrew Ambulance Brigades
V. Grisogono, *Sports Injuries: A Self Help Guide* (John Murray) 1984
N. Harris, J. Lovesey and C. Oram, *Sports Health Handbook* (World's Work Ltd) 1982
S. Miles (ed.), *Baillière's handbook of first aid*, 6th ed. (Baillière, Tindall & Cassell)
A. S. Playfair, *Modern first aid* (Hamlyn) 1979
The Red Cross, *Practical First Aid—a basic guide to emergency aid for home, school and work* (The Red Cross/Dorling Kindersley) 1984
St John's Ambulance Association and Brigade, *First aid—the authorised manual*, 3rd ed. 1977

APPENDIX F

B. Smith and G. Stevens, *The emergency book* (Penguin) 1982
P. N. Sperryn, *Sport and Medicine* (Butterworth) 1983
The Sports Council, *A catalogue of sports films* 1983
—, *A guide to the governing bodies of sport* 1981
A. Ward Gardner and P. J. Roylace, *New Essential First Aid* (Pan) 1982

PUBLICATIONS OF GENERAL INTEREST

Central Council of Physical Recreation, annual reports
Club Mirror (monthly newspaper)
Club Secretary (monthly magazine)
Governing bodies of sport: magazines, handbooks and annual reports
Institute of Leisure and Amenity Management, *The Leisure Manager* (monthly magazine)
The Sports Council, annual reports and *Sport and Leisure* (bi-monthly magazine)
Trade journals and magazines

Appendix G
Legal Precedents

A list of actions concerning sport and sports clubs mentioned in Chapter Five, Sports Clubs and the Law.

1. Brown v. Lewis (1896). Ref: Times Law Reports 455
2. Francis v. Cockerell (1870). Ref: Times Law Reports 455
3. Murray v. Haringay Arena (1951). Ref: 2 King's Bench (Law Reports)
4. Wooldridge v. Sumner (1963). Ref: 2 Queen's Bench (Law Reports) 2
5. Lewis v. Brookshaw (1970). Ref: *New Law Journal*, 30 April 1970, Vol. 120. p. 413
6. Gilbert v. Grundy (1978). Ref: *The Sunday Telegraph*, 31 July 1978, p. 31
7. R v. Billingshurst (1978). Ref: *The Daily Telegraph*, 15 June 1978, p. 3
8. Payne & Payne v. Maple Leaf Gardens Ltd (1949). Ref: Dominion Law Reports 369 (Canada)

Index

storage areas, 116
subscription levy, 34
subscriptions, 34–8

taxes, 49, 66–8
technique, 154
technological advice, 125–6
television and radio, 130
tobacco and cigarettes, sale of, 49
toilets, 117
Town and Country Planning Act
    1971, 137
training, 163
travel, 77–8
treasurer, 20–1
Truck Acts 1831–1940, 144
trusts or charities, 65, 97, 99

umpires, 160, 165
Unfair Contract Terms Act 1977, 145

Urban Programme, 91
use of facilities by outside groups,
    56–7

value added tax (VAT), 49, 66
vandalism, 56, 75, 116
Variety Club of Great Britain, 99
Voluntary Project Programme, 95
Voluntary Services Unit, 95

Wages Councils, 69, 144
Wages Councils Act 1959, 144
wages and National Insurance, 68
warm-up and warm-down, 163
water authorities, 90, 96
water and drainage, 66
Wolfson Foundation, 100
Working Men's Clubs, 29

Young Workers' Scheme, 91